Try Common Sense

TRY COMMON SENSE

REPLACING THE FAILED IDEOLOGIES OF RIGHT AND LEFT

PHILIP K. HOWARD

W. W. NORTON & COMPANY

Independent Publishers Since 1923

New York | London

Copyright © 2007 by W.H. Auden, renewed
Reprinted by permission of Curtis Brow, Ltd.

"Horae Canonicae" from COLLECTED POEMS by W.H. Auden, copyright © 1976 by
Edward Mendelson, William Meredith and Monroe K. Spears, Executors of the Estate of
W.H. Auden. Used by permission of Random House, an imprint and division of Penguin
Random House LLC. All rights reserved.

Edna St. Vincent Millay, excerpt from "We have gone too far; we do not know how to stop;
impetus" from *Collected Poems*. Copyright 1940, © 1968 by Edna St. Vincent Millay and
Normal Millay Ellis. Reprinted with the permission of The Permissions Company, Inc., on
behalf of Holly Peppe, Literary Executor, The Millay Society, www.millay.org.

For information about permission to reproduce selections from this book, write to
Permissions, W. W. Norton & Company, Inc., 500 Fifth Avenue, New York, NY 10110

For information about special discounts for bulk purchases, please contact
W. W. Norton Special Sales at specialsales@wwnorton.com or 800-233-4830

Manufacturing by Lake Book Manufacturing
Book design by Chris Welch Design
Production manager: Julia Druskin

ISBN 978-1-324-00176-8

W. W. Norton & Company, Inc., 500 Fifth Avenue, New York, N.Y. 10110
www.wwnorton.com

W. W. Norton & Company Ltd., 15 Carlisle Street, London W1D 3BS

1 2 3 4 5 6 7 8 9 0

WITH GRATITUDE TO MY EARLY MENTORS
EUGENE WIGNER, KENT BARWICK, JOHN WARDEN,
AND ARTHUR SCHLESINGER, JR.

CONTENTS

INTRODUCTION

The 2016 election of Donald Trump showed, sooner than I expected, that voters are so fed up with overbearing government that they were ready for change at almost any price. But the tepid response by both parties surprised me more. After continuing to work through 2017 with the new administration and Congress to try to unstick the gears, I realized that persuading Washington is hopeless. The political parties just continue to sow partisan distrust instead of dealing with the root causes of voter anger. They compete by dividing society, and rely on the lack of credible political alternatives to take turns in power without actually taking responsibility to fix things. Their duopoly has settled into a predictable pattern: First you fail, then I fail.

Fixing Washington requires more than new leaders and new variations on partisan orthodoxies. It requires a new governing vision, propelled by public demand, for a basic overhaul of how government works. Reforming the current system will not be sufficient. Pretty much everything run by government is broken—schools are bad, health-care costs are out of control, regulation is impractical, infrastructure is decrepit, Washington is a feeding trough, . . . and neither Congress nor the president has a coherent vision of how to deal with any of these problems.

What's needed is a governing philosophy that re-empowers people to make practical choices. The parties argue about ideological abstractions when voter anger stems mainly from the stifling of sensible decisions throughout society.

Most people want to be practical in their daily encounters. We want the teacher or principal to listen to us, and have the ability to make a decision. We want elected leaders to deal with problems, and to try something else if the first solution doesn't work. We want a workplace where people want to pitch in and expect others to do the same. Letting people make practical choices is not a radical idea, of course. The Framers embraced this practical ideal and created a framework in which Americans could pursue their dreams and live their values.

Practicality requires one essential element: people must be free to take responsibility. Only a person on the spot, not a bureaucratic rulebook, can make choices that are practical and fair. That's not possible in modern government, which is organized to dictate correct choices in advance.

In this book I propose a new governing philosophy built on the bedrock of human responsibility and accountability. Law should set goals and governing principles, and leave implementation to people on the ground. To get things done, and feel good about themselves, people need to have more ownership of their daily choices. Their choices can be judged, but they can't be dictated in advance without causing alienation and failure. This requires a radical simplification of government, area by area.

Under this new governing philosophy, choices can be practical. People are empowered to take into account all the circumstances. Instead of uniformity, it encourages local differences. Instead of aspiring to avoid disagreement with "clear rules" set out in advance, it encourages argument over what's right. Instead of legal entitlements, it aspires to balance different interests. Instead of requiring objective proof, it allows people to make judgments based on their perceptions and values. Instead of judging people by legalistic compliance, it judges them by the results they achieve and their good faith.

America's current governing philosophy, created after the 1960s, dictates governing choices out of a huge legal machine, programmed with about 150 million words for federal law. Its one virtue, at least to people in Washington, is that it absolves them from having to take responsibility for how things actually work. What keeps it in place, despite its failure, is distrust.

America's two political parties are mighty engines of distrust. They draw ideological lines in the sand and thrive on polarization. Their solutions are either negative (Stop the regulator!) or self-interested (Give me my rights!). What they share is a governing philosophy grounded in distrust of people taking responsibility. The worse things work, the more reluctant we are to let anyone make decisions. Just imagine the abuses if teachers, inspectors, managers, and citizens were able to work out disagreements, and be accountable for how they did.

The decline of responsibility in Washington over the past fifty years has been accompanied by a rise in apathy and selfishness in the broader culture. Working for the common good seems naïve. Why bother to get involved? You can't make a difference anyway. A culture not tethered to responsible individuals is soon dominated by self-interested demands. The common good? Just kick that can down the road.

There's a lot to talk about here, but the first hurdle is to convince you that proposing a practical governing philosophy is itself a practical exercise. Washington, we all know, is not exactly responsive to voter needs. It can barely pass a budget, much less overhaul its governing structure. Its defective approach to governing is compounded by a vacuum of leadership. It is unlikely to fix this problem. Change will only come from the outside. Historic shifts in our governing structure always require overwhelming public pressure—as, for example, in the Great Depression or the civil rights movement in the 1960s.

Public demand for a new governing philosophy can impact the culture long before the structures collapse of their own weight. Values have their own power. Having a principled basis for practical decisions may inspire people to make them. It will provide a vocabulary for dealing with daily idiocies in schools, hospitals, and government. Today people are awash in endless rules and legalisms, without any principled basis for getting to a reasonable solution.

Find any good public program, or, indeed, any successful enterprise, and you will see people who make choices based on what they think is right and sensible—not rote compliance. Embracing a public philosophy of practical responsibility will bring these outlaws out of the shadows and up on a pedestal of legitimacy and honor. It will encourage others to follow their lead. Americans can act like Americans again.

A new philosophy will also inspire a new generation of political leaders with a clear vision for change. Today, no leader has any credible way of explaining public failures, much less fixing them.

Am I just tilting at windmills? I've written about the failures of modern government in my prior books, and, in *The Rule of Nobody* (2014), described how a rigid conception of the Rule of Law removes the human authority needed to make common choices. The unintended effect is gridlock throughout society. I wrote that a voter backlash against the overbearing and mindless bureaucracy was inevitable.

Now that the backlash has started, America needs a new vision of how to govern. The time is now. The parties have left behind a vacuum that will be filled by something. Waiting for someone else to fill that vacuum is perilous. Unreliable leaders and bad ideas emerge when the public feels frustrated and marginalized. Unless they see a responsible path to a better future, people will grab hold of almost any alternative to the current chaos.

America may be prosperous, but not evenly, and many Americans are fearful. The employment base of communities can disappear overnight, replaced by robots or cheap labor overseas. What's left in the service sector are, increasingly, dead-end jobs that often don't get a worker past the poverty line. After a century of economic advancement, many Americans feel they are back in the fields again, meeting production quotas in mindless jobs. Many Americans don't find meaning in their work, or in their community. They are losing hope of a better future for their children. Americans are largely alienated from democratic governance. They don't matter to Washington, and they know it.

In his 1939 book, *The End of Economic Man*, Peter Drucker argued that the rise of fascism in Germany and Italy was fueled by absence of a governing vision that might counteract the

impersonal forces of the depression. The "old order has ceased
to have validity and reality. . . . But there has emerged no new
order which would have brought a new basis of belief."

Hitler and Mussolini offered a vision of totalitarian organization. The trains ran on time. Power became "its own justification." The establishment didn't like the fanaticism, but went
along because they had no better idea. Sure, as Drucker paro-
died the German establishment, the fascists "occasionally 'go
too far' in revolutionary zeal," but they were bringing people
together and providing employment. Never mind that the jobs
were for rearmament, and that the togetherness was achieved
by whipping people into a frenzy against Jews.

Facts no longer matter when people are consumed with
hatred or fear. Drucker observed that it was "useless to point
out that Mr. Roosevelt's name was not originally Rosenfeld" or
that an official inquiry concluded that the communists did not
set fire to the Reichstag. "All these lies must remain the official
truth in Germany."

A movement built on hatred was doomed to fail, Drucker
argued, because it has no positive governing vision for a healthy
society. Appeasement and peace were also impossible because
Hitler's only reason for existence was to attack an enemy.

Drucker's book was reviewed in England by a washed-up
politician who concluded that Drucker "successfully links
the dictatorships . . . with that absence of a working philosophy" elsewhere. People "seek refuge in [dictatorships] not
because they believe in them but because anything is better
than the present chaos." As the war escalated from 1939 to
1940, the columnist kept referring to Drucker's book while

arguing for a principled vision of a free society that must oppose the evil fanaticism of Hitler and Mussolini.

The washed-up columnist was Winston Churchill. When Hitler invaded the Low Countries, Parliament asked Churchill, then sixty-five years old, to lead the nation. What Winston Churchill provided, Drucker wrote thirty years later, was "moral authority, belief in values, and faith in the rightness of rational action."

Europe in 1939 is not America in 2019. Our stock market is booming, unemployment is low, and American culture is resilient. But it's hard not to notice a few similarities. Facts have lost their moral force. Can you prove Obama was born in the United States? Political leaders stir up public support not with visions of hope, but by attacking people and institutions that, until yesterday, were pillars of society. Is the FBI really corrupt? Americans, fearful of the future, retreat into echo chambers of paranoia and escalating hatred.

"Every organized society," Drucker wrote, "is built upon a concept of the nature of man and of his function and place in society." Americans feel increasingly isolated and powerless. That's dangerous.

PART I

REPLACING A FAILED PHILOSOPHY

"The evil of our times consists . . . in a kind of
degradation, indeed in a pulverization, of the
fundamental uniqueness of each
human person."

—Karol Wojtyla (Pope John Paul II)

MODERN GOVERNMENT IS DISCONNECTED FROM
the needs and capabilities of real people. Instead of honoring
"the fundamental uniqueness of each human person," it dictates uniform public choices at a granular level, applying to all
people. The relevant question in public interactions is not what
a person needs or believes, but what the rule requires.

The detail of American regulation is overwhelming, serving
no public purpose other than the quest for complete uniformity
even in small choices. It far exceeds any conception of human
scale. No one, certainly not citizens and small business, can

keep all this regulation straight. Steve Eder in *The New York Times* in 2017 provided a snapshot of how one family-owned apple orchard, Indian Ladder Farms in upstate New York, must comply with about 5,000 rules from seventeen different regulatory programs dealing with orchards. Some of these regulations are astonishingly impractical—such as a requirement to walk around the orchard every morning to check for mouse and deer droppings ("the equivalent of finding an earring in the orchard"). Another food safety rule requires that the cart filled with picked apples must be covered with a cloth for the trip to the barn (a journey of a few minutes) to protect against droppings from a bird flying by. The apples have been exposed to the birds for five months while growing on the tree, so it's unclear what purpose is served.

Indian Ladder Farms has never had a serious regulatory violation, but that doesn't prevent inspectors from different agencies from swooping in from time to time, and demanding reams of paperwork and issuing sanctions for foot faults. The regulators think they're just doing their job. Most people see it as piling on.

Governing by uniform rules has spawned a public culture where officials, conditioned always to look to law, feel disempowered from doing what they know is right. In one small incident, a school board in Rhode Island refused to accept a donation of a prom dress for a student who couldn't afford one because "if the school board officially accepted the dress . . . it would become school department property," and therefore could not be just given away to the girl.

Governing today is as thoughtful as airport security screening—where we trudge through lines and dedicate time and resources to comply with rigid requirements, and then are pulled aside to be searched if, say, we left a nickel in our pocket. We resent the bureaucrats who conduct these regulatory searches, but they're not allowed to use their judgment either. Life in the global economy roars by, with all its challenges and opportunities, while Americans stand in line, trying to comply with lengthy legal checklists.

Mindless application of law commonly skews choices away from what people know is right. In 2016, two volunteer firefighters in Stafford, Virginia, responded to an emergency call at a McDonalds, where an eighteen-month-old child was turning blue from a seizure. They immediately put her in the fire truck and took her to the hospital, administering oxygen along the way, and got there within thirteen minutes of the original call. The County's reaction to the firemen saving the child's life was to suspend them from further volunteer duty. The disciplinary logic was that the volunteer firefighters acted illegally because the fire truck was certified only as a "non-transport unit" and lacked "proper restraints" for carrying victims.

Not all public safety officers are heroes, and good government is impossible unless officials can make judgments about accountability. But, here as well, rules prevent officials from doing what's right. As a result of the "Black Lives Matter" movement, Reuters compiled a report on police officers with records of repeatedly abusing innocent people. One officer brutally beat up a college student who was sitting on a bench with friends, for the alleged crime of drinking a beer in public. That officer had been the subject of forty complaints of misconduct and similar abuses. But most bad officers, Reuters found, could not be dismissed. Why? The rule in public union contracts requires that prior complaints and infractions be expunged from the record, in some jurisdictions after a few months, so it's almost impossible for supervisors to terminate repeat offenders. No conceivable public purpose is served by whitewashing the record of abusive officers. But that's the rule.

American government is failing for the same reason it has estranged its citizens: it preempts the active intelligence and moral judgments of people on the ground. At this point, legal justification has become an obsession within our public culture, consistently making smart people act like they're brain dead.

In the spring of 2018, the Trump administration announced a "zero tolerance" policy for immigrants crossing the border illegally. Several thousand people were put in jail immediately when caught, and separated from their children, including infants, who were put in shelters. "We don't want to separate families, but we don't want families to come to the border illegally," Attorney General Jeff Sessions said: "This is just the way the world works." Columnist George Will ridiculed the administration for "an absence of judgment, institutionalized." Which is worse from a moral standpoint—entering a country illegally or separating young children from their parents?

Concerned about the fate of the separated children, the president of American Academy of Pediatrics, Dr. Colleen Kraft, visited a detention center with sixty children in Texas. There she saw caregivers doing their best to try to care for the children. She observed "a little girl no older than 2, screaming and pounding her fists on a mat." But the caregiver was also frustrated "because as much as she wanted to console the little girl, she couldn't touch, hold or pick her up to let her know everything would be all right." That was the rule: "They're not allowed to touch the children." The human instinct for caring and sympathy was pulverized by law.

How did American government get to the point where practicality and morality are no longer relevant—where regulations are so dense that people can't understand them; where firemen who save lives are fired and abusive policemen are protected; where our national leaders lose sight of basic morality in the name of legal "zero tolerance?" The public uproar over separating families from their children eventually caused the Trump administration to back down. But no one has changed the rule that bans picking up a crying toddler.

The function and place of individuals in American public life, in one sense, could hardly be clearer: What you believe doesn't matter. What the official believes doesn't matter either.

When Michael Bloomberg was considering running for president in the 2012 election, he suggested that fixing Washington was a "management problem." I am an admirer of Bloomberg, who was an exemplary mayor of New York City. But American government is suffering from a failure of philosophy, not merely bad management. Governing requires human judgment, not rote compliance. America needs a governing philosophy that gives responsibility, and meaning, back to each citizen and each official.

1
America the Practical

"The Founding Fathers ... were extremely
pragmatic in their day-to-day politics. ... All
they wanted was a solution that would do
the job in hand—provided it could be fitted
into the broad frame of principles."

—Peter Drucker

Americans are a practical people. Where other cultures got bogged down in preconceived ways of doing things, Americans would adapt. If this doesn't work, try that. Americans have a bias for action. We didn't calculate our way to success, we forged ahead. Trial and error could be our national motto. Failure is not bad, but essential; it's how we learn what doesn't work.

Practicality is baked into American culture. Making things happen in our own way provides meaning and self-fulfillment. We see a challenge, and want to deal with it. We see a need, and want to fill it. People have ownership of daily choices.

But not in Washington. A sensible solution is staring us in the face. There it is, needing only a person to act on it. Why can't government be practical? That's the complaint I hear more than any other. Why don't bureaucrats and legislators do what makes sense? Good government is impossible without practicality. Public choices must account for limited time and resources. Obsolete programs must be jettisoned to free up money and manpower for current needs. Timely approvals will maximize the benefits of new drugs and infrastructure. Teachers must balance the demands of one student against the needs of another. Regulators must respect the limited capacity of farmers and small businesses to deal with complex regulations.

Government's abject failure to make practical choices is not a matter of dispute. But it is typically debated as a matter of failed public policy. Republicans call for deregulation. Democrats call for more regulation and more funding. Meanwhile the actual cause of failure, the inability to be sensible in actual situations, is demonstrated to Americans on a daily basis. Worthwhile public goals emerge as scrap from the giant bureaucratic machinery. America spends more money on schools than almost any other country, with pathetic results. The failures of modern government are, overwhelmingly, failures of implementation.

What's missing in American government is the indispensable element of all human accomplishment: personal responsibility for results. Practicality is not just a matter of personal wisdom. Practicality requires giving officials responsibility to act sensibly. Officials must be on the hook to achieve public goals in a fair and effective way, visible to the affected public and accountable up the hierarchy.

Responsibility is one of those words, like freedom or rights, that is so worn by overuse that it slips around the brain without imparting meaning. "Being responsible" often means to be less self-centered, as when do-gooders exhort us to remember that rights come with responsibilities. Responsibility in organization-speak has been degraded into a concept of compliance. Sure, I fulfilled my responsibility: I showed up on time; I followed the rules; gosh, it's too bad nothing got done.

Real responsibility, by contrast, is an active obligation to accomplish something concrete—a duty paired with authority to satisfy it. You have a goal. You must strive to achieve it. Responsibility means a person takes *ownership of results*. "The essential condition of responsibility," Nobel economist Friedrich Hayek observed, "is that it refer to circumstances that the individual can judge [and] to problems . . . whose solution he can . . . consider his own."

The three ingredients of responsibility are a goal, the authority to achieve it in your own way, and accountability to those around you. Without authority, responsibility is all talk and no action. Without accountability, responsibility will soon be replaced by red tape—no one will be given carte blanche.

To our modern sensibility, what's most radical here is that the responsible person can draw on his instincts and values, and engage in trial and error, to fulfill the public goal. Responsibility generally requires adapting to the circumstances—the concept of practicality. Practicality is mainly a local phenomenon, requiring decisions on the ground. No situation, no person, is quite the same. That's why practicality can't be preset in rules—it is the "practice" of people balancing and deciding on the spot.

Responsibility requires liberating people to draw on perceptions and instincts that have been vestigial for decades. Judging people by their character, for example, must be revived as a litmus test for public as well as private choices. Striving to avoid "being judgmental" about people is largely responsible for the epidemic of self-interest that is corroding our culture.

Giving officials responsibility was the organizing idea of our Constitution. Law allocates the scope of responsibility to designated officials and bodies, and gives other people the job of holding them accountable. As James Madison describes: "Responsibility, in order to be reasonable, must be limited to objects within the power of the responsible party, . . . of which a ready and proper judgment can be formed by the constituents."

To our modern sensibility, giving a person responsibility seems like an invitation to tyranny. But the spotlight of responsibility is actually the best protection against abuse, and also avoids the tyranny of mindless rules. The Framers considered it far safer to give one person responsibility than to disperse responsibility among several people. As Alexander Hamilton put it: "The sole and undivided responsibility of one man will naturally beget a livelier sense of duty and a more exact regard to reputation." Otherwise, Hamilton emphasized, responsibility can be "shifted from one to another with so much dexterity, and under such plausible appearances, that the public opinion is left in suspense about the real author." George Washington made the same point: "Whenever one person is found adequate to the discharge of a duty . . . it is worse executed by two persons, and scarcely done at all if three or more are employed."

Remaking the structure of government to revive responsibility is not as daunting as you might think. It's a lot easier to create a simple framework of goals and governing principles than to write thousand-page rulebooks dictating how to do things. Governing by goals is also more coherent, for citizens as well as officials. There's no mystery in understanding the public mandate when the dispositive question in most situations should be: "What's the right thing to do here?"

Like deposing an aging dictator, restoring practicality to Washington requires a clean break. We must abandon the philosophy of dictating uniform public choices in tiny detail, with its huge oppressive bureaucracy, and restore human responsibility as the organizing principle of American government. Only by reconnecting the human links in the hierarchy of democracy can government be practical, moral, and responsive to citizen needs.

2

The Fixation
on Correctness

"The nature of despotic power in
democratic ages is not to be fierce or
cruel, but minute and meddling."

—Alexis de Tocqueville

Washington has given up on governing. It doesn't
fix programs that everyone knows have long been
broken. It doesn't respond to public anger at Big
Brother breathing down our necks in schools, hospitals, and
the workplace. What it touts as major reforms are usually just
tweaks in programs that are overdue for complete overhauls.

Most Americans want Washington to change how it works.
But attacking Washington is like punching into fog. There's no
clear path to reform. It's hard to find any coherent vision of how
government could work differently.

Trump promised to "drain the swamp." That sounds good,
but how does government make decisions the next day, after
there's dry land in Washington? I can't find his idea on how
public schools will be run better, or health-care costs reined in,
or obsolete subsidies eliminated.

Let's look to our leaders in Congress. What is the governing vision of Mitch McConnell? Asking the question seems absurd, like the beginning of a comedy skit. How about Nancy Pelosi? They're not trying to fix Washington. They don't even think about it. They're too busy blaming each other for Washington's failures.

While I find both parties hateful, I also think that partisan politics are a symptom of the deeper flaw in our governing system. Politicians point fingers because they've given up trying to fix things. There's plenty of room for compromise between conservative and liberal ideologies, between liberating individual initiative and protecting individual rights. What's missing is a theory of action.

There is one assumption that the parties happen to agree upon, part of an unstated frame of reference for modern public culture. The shared assumption is this: whatever government does, it should do with tight controls. The goal is to avoid mistakes and abuses. That's why rules are so prescriptive, so that neither officials nor citizens have any leeway for bad judgment. For unavoidable decisions—say, giving a permit—the person with responsibility must be able to demonstrate, by objective proof, that the choice was correct. The motivation is mutual distrust: conservatives want to restrict officials, and liberals want to shackle businessmen.

This reverence for tight legal controls over every public choice is embedded in political philosophies of both sides. "Individual rights" against what? Against decisions by people with authority. Protect individual freedom against what? Against government authority.

The worse Washington works, the tighter the grip on public

choices. Washington may not work well but, by God, anything it does must pass through the eye of a legal needle.

This operating philosophy of modern government is a comparatively recent innovation, as I will discuss. But it's been around long enough that, with a little effort, we can put it in a jar and evaluate it as a scientist would describe any other experiment.

Its core premise is this: every public decision must be correct. The person making the decision must be able to demonstrate its correctness—either by compliance with a rule or metric, or by objective evidence. This philosophy was never given a name, probably because it seemed so obviously virtuous.

I'll call it the "philosophy of correctness." Its drive for purity in public choices is related to the cultural norm called "political correctness," but is much broader. The broader philosophy of correctness dictates decisions, not just how to talk about certain issues. Correctness requires that public choices must be demonstrably proper by reference to some objective measure. At long last, government would work as it should. After millennia of humans trying to govern themselves, our generation thought it had found the magic key to good government.

American government today is a giant, intricate edifice dedicated to the principle of correctness. All day long, Americans in schools, hospitals, and the workplace are trained to ask themselves: "Can I prove that what I'm about to do is legally correct?"

This philosophy of correctness has failed. Indeed, it should go down in history as the most unrealistic governing philosophy since Soviet central planning. The proof is in the pudding. Government has gotten progressively more inept since the 1960s. Society meanwhile has splintered into factions at war over abstract values when, most of the time, their frustrations stem from the inability to make practical choices on the spot.

Practically every encounter with government provides another story of the real-life peg not fitting the precision-made bureaucratic hole. J. D. Vance, the author of *Hillbilly Elegy*, attributes his unlikely path—from son of a drug addict mother to Yale Law School—to his upbringing by his grandparents. Today, he observes, his grandparents would likely be barred from taking him in unless they had been certified by the state. His fiercely proud and profane grandparents were unlikely to have tolerated, much less passed, such a bureaucratic screening.

What's missing is basic: people aren't allowed to make decisions. Trace any frustration, or waste, or roadblock back through the chain of the command and what you will find, in nine out of ten cases, are officials and citizens who feel disempowered to do what's right. Why did permitting approval to raise the roadway of the Bayonne Bridge, a project with virtually no environmental impact, take five years and require an environmental review statement of 20,000 pages, including exhibits? No official had authority to draw the line when naysayers kept demanding more.

The breakdown of schools and other public institutions since the 1960s was caused not by underfunding, but by the collapse of authority by the people in charge. The evidence is overwhelming. The link between human disempowerment and school failure is vividly presented in Gerald Grant's case study, *The World We Created at Hamilton High*. The statistical evidence connecting the rise of due process with the decline of order in schools is provided in Richard Arum's study, *Judging School Discipline*. The need to cull bad teachers is highlighted by the evidence of intangible distinctions among effective and ineffective teachers in Philip Jackson's study, *The Moral Life of Schools*. The personal leadership needed to build and maintain a healthy school culture is described in practically every study of good schools, including Sara Lawrence-Lightfoot's *The Good High School*.

Correctness was doomed to fail. Life is too complex for a correct system. People are unique, and can only be organized so much. There's no such thing as being a correct teacher or a correct factory. Circumstances always differ. Choices all involve trade-offs. Timing, resources, needs, passions, and other variables are infinitely complex, but the mold is fixed.

The theory, taken from the rationalist tradition of Enlightenment thinkers such as Descartes, was to protect against bad government choices by extruding them through a mold of correctness. The actual effect is constant pain and failure, not merely for government but throughout society. Telling government exactly how to regulate also, unfortunately, tells citizens exactly how to comply. That's why it grates on our nerves. Correctness forces Americans to contort themselves, like legal Houdinis, to make obvious daily choices.

Correctness now permeates the culture. Its utopian beacon casts a harsh light on anything that goes wrong, which must be the result of someone acting incorrectly. Any accident is an affront to proper planning. What Nassim Taleb calls the "Soviet-Harvard delusion" drives people towards controlling every possible activity. Children's play has been transformed; "neurotically overprotective parents," Taleb explains, preclude the trial and error needed for children to learn how to be resourceful as adults.

The ironies of correctness are many—what is called pure is usually toxic. The quest for neutral morality has resulted in an amoral culture, where rules prevent doing what is right. In one incident, firemen in Washington stood by and refused to help a victim right in front of their station because, as they explained to onlookers pleading for their help, the rules said that the proper procedure is to call 911. The man died. School administrators in New York refused to call 911 when a high school student had a stroke because a new school rule prohibited calling 911 (a rule intended to prevent overreliance on police for discipline). The girl survived.

Legal rigidity invites people to find openings for self-interest. Like water through a crack, selfishness saturates society through the fissures of this rigid system. Parties to a contract seize on any sliver of ambiguity to avoid performing their side of the deal. College students now have the idea that unsettling literature or ideas should be barred. Don't you know that King Lear was a misogynist? The reach of correctness is limited only by the imagination of the self-perceived victim.

Life cannot be reduced to an abstract ideal of correctness. Conflict and adversity are unavoidable features of the human condition. The choices needed to get things done, and to be moral, and to promote joint activities, cannot be compartmentalized into correct or not. Every choice has costs and risks.

Governing is not an abstraction either. It requires decisions— to protect clean water, to oversee safety in numerous activities, and to provide social services. These governing activities are intended to enhance everyone's freedom by providing common goods and protecting against abuse. But it is not sufficient for government to have a pure heart when mandating and funding these goals; it must implement them sensibly and fairly. Whether government succeeds tolerably is determined not by a theory, but by the reality of how it works on the ground. That, in turn, hinges on the choices made in each situation—whether by a teacher, an inspector, or the president.

Just as correctness frustrates our daily choices, so too it has immobilized Washington. Almost any new choice conflicts with some rule somewhere. Multiple legal pathways of rules and congressional committees are in constant conflict, with no hierarchy of authority to resolve them. Only by ignoring rules can officials get things done. Political scientist Francis Fukuyama calls modern government a "vetocracy"—anyone can veto anything. It seems to me more like a massive short circuit. For special interests, it couldn't be easier to stop reform: just jump a few wires of overlapping jurisdiction and inconsistent regulations and, poof, reform goes up in smoke.

At this point, Washington is run by inertia. No one wants responsibility for actual results. Compliance is a lot easier than hard choices. Political leaders rail against the government they are elected to lead. Republicans have perfected the art of being the party of opposition even when they're in control. Meanwhile, Washington is on automatic pilot, plowing forward as the accumulated laws and regulations require. The political noise is all for show.

Electing new leaders can't fix this defect in modern American government, any more than I could fix a computer with a melted circuit board. America needs a governing framework that reconnects real people with actual results.

3

Back to Basics

ALLOCATE SCOPE OF RESPONSIBILITY

> "A free society rests on the freedom
> to make responsible decisions."
>
> —Peter Drucker

Our goal was to create a kind of automatic government, where law would operate as a software program. But shackling officials with detailed rules, paradoxically, resulted in disempowering ourselves. We stripped the gears by which joint action is possible. In our quest for greater personal autonomy from official choices, we instead "find ourselves at the mercy of these mysterious, impersonal, and remote mechanisms that we have ourselves created," Philip Slater observed: "Their indifference is a reflection of our own."

I propose a new approach that happens to be the old approach: Organize government by scope of responsibility. Radically simplify law into goals and guiding principles, and give designated officials responsibility to meet public goals sensibly and fairly. Give other officials responsibility to judge how they do. Instead of legal tentacles wrapped tight around each choice, law becomes a fence around a corral within which a wide range of choices is available. For officials, law defines their jurisdiction and gives room to make sensible choices. For citizens, law defines outer boundaries of a broad field of freedom and does not interfere with daily choices as long as they don't transcend the boundaries safeguarded by officials.

Common choices are needed for society to move forward. Giving officials flexibility to take this responsibility has the paradoxical effect of empowering all around them, including citizens. "Power is one of those rare commodities," William O'Brien noted, where "the more you give away, the more influence you retain." The teacher is able to use the personal resources of personality, experience, willpower to make students excited about learning. The principal decides whether she is doing a good job. Another official or committee decides whether the principal is a good leader, and whether her judgments are fair. Instead of being stymied by mindless bureaucracy, parents now can deal with educators who are empowered to act as they think is sensible and fair. The parents' ideas will matter only if someone can act on them.

Allocating responsibility to identifiable officials radically alters today's governing dynamic. Instead of tiptoeing in the legal minefield and speaking in bureaucratic gobbledygook, people with responsibility find themselves in the spotlight, speaking the plain language of right and wrong. Other people affected by decisions now have a responsible official to talk with and try to persuade. Competing approaches are crystalized. Instead of punching at fog, citizens and other officials can punch at an identifiable person. When officials act unreasonably, they can be held accountable by their superiors in a democratic hierarchy—and ultimately by voters.

Apologists for the bureaucratic state suggest that without detailed rules people will disagree on the best decision. Of course, people have different goals and viewpoints. Conflict is sown in human nature, as the Framers emphasized. Conflict is useful as well as unavoidable; it is conflict that gives democracy its energy and relevance. By providing a hierarchy of authority to resolve conflict, democracy has a gravitational pull, bringing disparate parties together to argue their position. The inevitable differences are far healthier than avoiding responsibility with disingenuous legal arguments ("The rule doesn't allow it"; "Just do another study"). As sociologist Lewis Coser describes, conflict not only enhances mutual understanding, but also acts as a "safety valve" and provides a mechanism for "clearing the air." Even when people don't get their way, legal philosopher Jeremy Waldron says, they feel respected that a real person heard them out.

Conflict is unhealthy only in the context of rigid systems, Coser found, such as in tangled bureaucracies that are unable to respond to human needs. Citizens today find themselves dealing with legal requirements that matter to no one—such as doing a traffic study for a bridge repair that isn't affecting traffic. A predictable outcome of mindless legalisms, as Orwell described in *1984*, is that people who "[keep] the small rules" can get away with whatever they want. Terrible officials, teachers, and contractors keep their jobs because they fill out the forms correctly. Rigid systems are besieged by people demanding their rights. Your rights? What about my rights? Those conflicts, Coser concluded, can "tear apart" a society.

"The greatest menace to freedom," Justice Louis Brandeis

said, "is an inert people." Correctness *aspires* to an inert people, and, indeed, to an inert government: just follow the rules.

Reviving responsibility also puts public decisions back on course towards the common good. Instead of trying to mollify each claimant's legal argument, the duty of the responsible official is to act for the good of all. Public choices should aspire to be sensible and moral for society as a whole. Claimants must frame their arguments as responsible public choices, not entitlements. Accountability must be judged against the official's responsibility to society, not pleasing the squeaky wheels.

Rebuilding government by scope of responsibility will rebalance the scales away from the lowest common denominator. For example, in deciding whether to approve new infrastructure—say, an intermodal freight transfer facility—the disruption of a local neighborhood is certainly a relevant factor. But the more important goal is probably eliminating inefficient, polluting bottlenecks. Some official must have the job of approving that facility in the twenty-first century, just as two hundred years ago Governor DeWitt Clinton approved the Erie Canal, despite ridicule about "Clinton's big ditch." Public choices will always hurt someone; the question is whether the overall benefit is greater. The Erie Canal, for example, cut transportation costs by 95 percent and transformed the New York economy. New infrastructure in our generation will also provide broad benefits. Officials must have the authority to make these choices.

Regulating fairly also requires judgment, and a hierarchy to resolve conflict. A safety inspector, for example, has the job of protecting against unsafe workplaces, and it is clearly within the scope of his responsibility to call out, say, an unguarded rotary saw. The factory foreman can make his case by making practical arguments: "The equipment is only used a few times per year, always with extra precautions. We've never had an accident with it." If the inspector is unconvinced and orders a change, the factory can contest his decision up to a supervisor, and, if it feels really strongly, to a court. If the inspector is out of bounds, he too should be accountable. In all these permutations, however, the focus is on the reasonable exercise of responsibility to meet the public goal.

To use a nongovernmental example: is assigning *King Lear* within the reasonable scope of the English professor's responsibility? If so, it doesn't matter if some students think *King Lear* is misogynistic. They don't have to take the class. They can transfer to another college. It's a free country. What they shouldn't be allowed to do, in pursuit of their self-appointed rights, is remove the freedom of the professor to assign a respected literary text and remove the freedom of other students to study *King Lear*.

Reformers for fifty years have been unable to conceive of letting an official take responsibility to make a decision just because it seems right. Official responsibility seems too dangerous. We want rules or other "proof." But preempting judgment with legal dictates backfired. "The idea of law," Yale law professor Grant Gilmore concluded, was "ridiculously oversold." Instead of enhancing our freedom, all this law left loopholes that are filled by selfish people with no responsibility for the common good. To add insult to injury, the legal tangle disempowers everyone else from balancing different interests. Lousy schools, runaway healthcare costs, and overbearing regulation are all caused by the absence of people making practical choices on the ground.

That's why the only solution is to put humans in charge again. As Madison and Hamilton explained, responsibility is the least dangerous system. An "official's discretion," legal philosopher Ronald Dworkin explained, does not mean "that he is free to decide without recourse to standards of sense and fairness."

Letting real people take responsibility for results may seem self-evident and simplistic. The utopians who spent half a century writing detailed codes probably wouldn't describe their mission as eliminating human agency or responsibility. They just wanted to be sure humans didn't make mistakes. Their conceit was that decisions in advance would make for a better society. By controlling choices to avoid mistakes, however, they achieved the opposite: correctness guaranteed mistakes, and, as I describe now, also unwittingly destroyed the cognitive capacity for humans to succeed.

4

How Correctness Causes Failure and Alienation

"Nothing that's any good works by itself, just to please you. You got to make the damn thing work."

—Thomas Edison

Some evolutionary tendency drives humans to want to control choices. Rules are a kind of security blanket. Hume noted that people are "mightily addicted to rules." Coming out of the upheavals of the 1960s, it is perhaps understandable that people wanted a governing system that rescued them from having to take responsibility. People just wanted to take a deep breath after the riots and protests, and walk back out into a society where everyone just follows the rules, and conflict would be no more.

But it doesn't work. The rules don't avoid conflict; they just push it towards the parsing of legal language. Instead of arguing over the merits, people demand conflicting rights. Controlling choices by setting rules in advance causes many social ills, including putting society in a pressure cooker because there's no valve to relieve daily frustrations.

The core flaw of correctness, however, is its premise—that

there is a correct way of doing things. The reason to abandon this governing philosophy, notwithstanding our longing for rules, is that it guarantees failure while poisoning what is effective and noble about human aspiration. Choices dictated in advance never align with the kaleidoscope of situations that life presents to us every day.

Public Choices Involve Unavoidable Trade-Offs

The truth of any matter, a nineteenth-century historian observed, lies not at the center but at the edges, where it intersects with all other matters. Deciding what to do always involves tensions among competing goals and values, scarce resources and time constraints. "A decision . . . is rarely a choice between right and wrong," Peter Drucker observed. "It is at best a choice between 'almost right' and 'probably wrong.' "

Every choice has a cost. Caring for this patient in the emergency room means another patient has to wait. Building a high-voltage transmission line from a wind farm will reduce carbon pollution, but it may harm people who live under the line. Spending an extra dollar on special education means a dollar less for the arts program.

Striving too hard for one goal can undermine others. That's why experts can be so stupid: they're wearing blinders. Solving the one problem within their expertise will cause other problems elsewhere. Spending years preparing a perfect environmental review statement, for example, will generally harm the environment by delaying projects that alleviate polluting bottlenecks.

Fairness too requires personal judgments, because it involves weighing numerous factors in the situation. What's the right thing to do? It depends on the situation. Psychologist Barry Schwartz, in his book *Practical Wisdom*, tells a story of a janitor in a hospital who was confronted by a family member of a patient, who demanded that the hospital room be cleaned immediately. As it happens, the janitor had just cleaned that room. But, seeing that the family member was obviously upset, the janitor thought the man might feel better believing that he had helped in some way. So the janitor cleaned the room again.

Sometimes the choice is obvious: the person is bleeding, or the tunnel is about to collapse. Sometimes the choice requires weighing risks and benefits. But in almost every case, the choice can't be made in advance by a specific rule, and requires someone to make a judgment.

In *Descartes' Error*, Antonio Damasio describes people with lobotomies who retain their full powers of reasoning. But they can't make decisions. Their logic goes round and round, because they no longer have the capacity to make the value judgments needed to decide which is the best course.

Correctness has lobotomized government. Because every public choice involves trade-offs, there is no such thing as a demonstrably correct decision. So permitting takes years; procedures and forms multiply to address hypothetical harms; Congress accepts broken programs as if they were carved on stone tablets; and there are two sides to every story, even involving white supremacists.

The only way to make practical trade-offs is to let officials and citizens start making choices. People need to keep their eye on the ultimate public purpose. Rules veer off into preset directions that lead nowhere and, as I now discuss, slam the door to the smart part of human brains.

A Person, Not a System, Is the
Core Element of All Achievement

People succeed by instinct and intuition, not conscious reasoning or objective compliance. They perceive problems and opportunities, and react by trying this or that. In his study of human accomplishment, *Personal Knowledge,* Michael Polanyi refers to the "usual process of unconscious trial and error by which we *feel our way* to success . . . without specifiably knowing how we do it."

Daily decisions, even ones we consider simple, are too complex to dissect with any accuracy. We perceive a situation: how urgent is it; how upset is a person; does he seem honest? We react instinctively, often in seconds. Our judgment draws on a lifetime of experience that is impossible to unbundle. Skill and experience are two of the most powerful tools of human accomplishment, but they reside inarticulately in our subconscious. Our brain does it for us. People make most decisions based on what Polanyi calls "tacit knowledge," as opposed to conscious reasoning.

Rules and organization provide the framework, but implementation requires this subconscious focus. People get so immersed in a project that they are unaware of thinking or perceiving anything. They *become* the project.

One day I asked a former New York City Parks Commissioner, Henry Stern, how he was able to write two or three long essays each week on state politics, which I found unusually descriptive and perceptive. He said, "I don't know who writes it." I looked puzzled. "It just somehow comes out of my finger-tips onto the keyboard."

Doing anything successfully requires this immersion. We have a goal and we dive in, drawing on our own instincts, experience, and values. Philip Jackson's study of successful teachers shows how they make constant small choices to preside over a classroom in a way that engages students in learning, just as a skilled equestrian might ride a horse. W. H. Auden has a poem about it: "You need not see what someone is doing / to know if it is his vocation, / you have only to watch his eyes: a cook... a surgeon... a clerk / wear the same rapt expression, / forgetting themselves in a function."

All politics is local, it is said. The corollary is that all governing is personal. Daily interactions by government, Michael Lipsky described in *Street Level Bureaucracy*, "call for sensitive observation and judgment, which are not reducible to programmed formats." Herbert Kaufman's study of forest rangers in the 1950s reveals a regulatory framework of "guided discretion," which allowed rangers to achieve public goals in their own ways. Legislatures and agency heads can set goals, but wisdom boils down to judgments on the ground. Worker safety was enhanced in Maine when the senior federal regulator allowed factories to create their own safety plan instead of directing their energies to rote compliance.

Correctness doesn't honor the complexity of real life, and instead supplants ultimate goals with surrogates that are easier to evaluate: rules, metrics, and objective proof. The result is called goals-displacement: people lose sight of the ultimate purpose. Surgeons who were evaluated by mortality rate of patients, for example, just stopped accepting difficult cases, thus denying care to the patients who needed skilled surgeons the most.

Correctness also interferes with mental focus. People can't think of two things at once. In an experiment asking people to count the number of basketball passes in a video clip, most people did not notice when a gorilla walked across the screen. Focus on A, and you do not see B. Every day, all across America, government demands that we count basketballs and as a result we miss what's actually happening.

Achievement requires *not* justifying each step along the way. Before taking off, a pilot can go down a checklist to make sure he's not missing something. Once he's flying, he needs to focus on the job. More rules for firefighters, one study found, actually decreased their survival rates. "Too much reliance on rules," Barry Schwartz concludes, "can squeeze out the judgment that is necessary to do our work well."

Bureaucracy basically makes people stupid. It yanks people out of the smart part of their brain into the thin veneer of conscious logic. By forcing us to focus on the formal criteria instead of ultimate goals, it effectively shuts the door to the deep well of human skill, experience, and values.

Correctness Crushes the Human Spirit

Bureaucracy's greatest flaw is what it does to the human spirit. By preventing people from taking ownership for daily choices, bureaucracy leaves behind a trail of burned-out people.

Correctness replaces the joy of accomplishment with the drudgery of compliance. This is not a matter merely of inefficiency. Working is about the search "for daily meaning as well as daily bread," as Studs Terkel observed.

People who get into a "flow" of accomplishing things in their own way find that work is both invigorating and fulfilling. People are energized by the satisfaction of drawing on all their instincts to achieve wonderful things—teaching students, or healing patients, or overseeing health and safety in a way that's practical. Giving people ownership lets people make a difference. "Few things help an individual more than to place responsibility upon him," Booker T. Washington noted: "Every individual responds to confidence."

Constant justification, by contrast, is both demoralizing and exhausting. Because bureaucratic criteria cannot be internalized, they require conscious mental effort. People must turn away from their instincts and make themselves think about the rules. It's as if you're trying to drive somewhere and must constantly stop to explain which lanes you drove in and which gauges you checked to make sure the engine is okay, then do it again a few miles later. One of the principle causes of burnout is "lack of control"—"when workers have insufficient authority over their work or are unable to shape the work environment to be consistent with their values."

Bureaucracy, not hard work, is the main cause of burnout in modern life. People are whipsawed between failure and the demands to meet bureaucratic criteria that cause the failure. These contradictory signals, as with Pavlov's dogs, cause people to melt down. Bureaucracy is not merely inefficient. Bureaucracy is evil.

5

Forty Years of Marginal Reforms

"Nothing makes conditions more unbearable
than the knowledge that no effort of
ours can change them."

—Friedrich Hayek

America's governing philosophy began to leave the rails about five decades ago. The tumultuous decade of the 1960s resulted in important improvements to the social contract, including civil rights, environmental protection, and product safety. Almost as an afterthought, reformers also changed how government made decisions day to day. How could those prior practices have persisted for so long? While we're rewriting codes, reformers concluded, let's modernize the operating philosophy of government to preclude bad values ever again.

The philosophy of correctness was born. Law going forward would be like an instruction manual. Once law is perfectly clear, people will know exactly what to do. Bureaucrats would be more like workers on an assembly line. It's too dangerous to let officials be arbiters of right and wrong.

In the excitement over broad purification of government, the Supreme Court soon expanded the coverage of "due process"— the constitutional guarantee against the state improperly putting us in jail or taking our property—to daily management choices in schools and agencies. Any aggrieved person had the right to challenge a decision. The onus was on the official or employer to demonstrate that the decision was proper.

This shift in operating philosophy didn't generally make the front pages. I was in law school at the time, and pretty much everyone accepted these changes as prudent safeguards to abusive authority. Liberals were the main drivers of this new way of governing, as they were of the civil rights and environmental reforms. But conservatives saw a silver lining in detailed rules and rights. Clear lines would prevent officials from overstepping their bounds; business too could assert its rights. Who can be against "clear law" or "individual rights"?

Controlling small incidents of life was a dramatic expansion of legal reach beyond anything contemplated even by central planners. Only people who have spent their lives in a bureaucracy could think that it is helpful to mandate, as worker safety regulations do, seven pages of rules on ladders.

The idea of using law to redress ordinary disagreements in schools and the workplace soon infected the broader culture. People with a certain disposition, for example, began to threaten schools with claims that their child was treated unfairly, including over grades and extracurricular activities.

Almost immediately, Americans began to react against Big Brother breathing down their necks. A Harris poll in 1973 found that a "crisis of the most serious magnitude" was brewing in citizen dissatisfaction toward government—

a stark reversal of attitudes only a decade earlier. The poll
also revealed a sharp divergence between the discontent of
citizens and the complacency of political leaders, who saw no
serious issues with government.

In ten of the next eleven presidential elections, starting with Jimmy Carter in 1978, Americans elected outsider
candidates who promised to get government off our backs.
(George H. W. Bush was the sole exception, and he ran as Reagan's successor). None have succeeded.

Jimmy Carter came to Washington promising "to reorganize a Federal Government which had grown more preoccupied with its own bureaucratic needs than with those of
the people." With ideas from his domestic policy adviser Stu
Eizenstat, Carter deregulated several industries, including
airlines, trucking, railroads, and beer. He also initiated the
"senior executive service" to promote leadership within agencies. Carter had a sense that government was out of control,
leading to a broader sense of futility within society. He made
sunset laws a priority, writing to Congress in 1979: "Too many
Federal programs have been allowed to continue indefinitely
without examining whether they are accomplishing what they
were meant to do." But that effort stalled, and his ambitious
domestic agenda in his one term is largely overshadowed by
the Iran hostage crisis and the "stagflation" that doomed a
second term.

Ronald Reagan asserted in his first inaugural address that
"in this present crisis, government is not the solution to our
problem; government is the problem." By executive order in
1982 he created the Grace Commission, headed by corporate
leader J. Peter Grace, and tasked it with identifying waste in

the federal government—"a problem that's been 40 years in the making," Reagan declared. In January 1984, the Commission released a 656-page report proposing almost 2,500 reforms. Some of these were implemented by executive order, and Congress in 1988 authorized another of its cost-saving proposals—"base closing commissions" to make politically difficult decisions about which defense bases should be closed. The Commission focused on specific public management inefficiencies, however, not on how Washington governed.

Bill Clinton came to office advocating a "third way" to deal with government ineffectiveness, and empowered Vice President Al Gore to lead the charge. Instead of tackling a long list of inefficient programs, as the Grace Commission did, Gore's "reinventing government" program in the 1990s looked more broadly at how decisions were made. Procurement officers were given freedom to buy products off the shelf, at a fraction of the price paid through formal bids. Social Security provided customer service that won awards in the private sector. Forms were simplified and consolidated in some agencies. Several pilot projects showed how regulation would be more effective by focusing on results instead of compliance. At the end of the day, however, the improvements were more pronounced in internal administration of government than, for example, in making regulation and permitting more practical for citizens.

George W. Bush had been a practical and effective governor of Texas, but didn't seriously try to fix Washington. Where Al Gore might be mocked for being overly earnest in his pursuit of good government, George W. Bush under the tutelage of Karl Rove elevated the failure to fix problems as an accepted technique of cynical partisanship: propose an extreme bill that no moderate would support, and then blame the other side for not fixing the problem. I watched this firsthand when trying to lead medical malpractice reform. George W. Bush proposed a tort reform bill that he knew would fail, instead of a bill for reliable health courts that had bipartisan support. Then he blamed Democrats for not solving the problem.

Barack Obama was the freshest face since JFK, promising "change we can believe in." He appointed the prolific law professor Cass Sunstein to the job of "regulatory czar." Acting as a gatekeeper to new rules, Sunstein made new regulations less convoluted. Although he acknowledged the need for "retrospective review"—i.e., looking back at how regulations and programs actually work—Sunstein didn't do much to clean out decades of accumulated regulations and processes. Nor did Sunstein, who advocates using law to "nudge" people towards sensible decisions, tackle the disastrous behavioral effects of a rigid regulatory system. Sunstein is so prolific that, like the body of law itself, he can be cited for almost any proposition. Sometimes he talks about the need for flexibility; at other times he talks about the virtues of clear rules. When he left government, Sunstein wrote *Simpler*, a book detailing how he and Obama had simplified government. "I must have missed that," said one Washington insider.

Voters also missed Obama's simplification of Washington. In the 2016 election, eight million Obama supporters turned around and voted for Donald Trump. Trump has proved disruptive, as many voters wanted. Playing the bull in a china shop, Trump has undone what was legally handy—for example, rescinding many Obama executive orders. He has also stimulated business initiatives by the clear signal that federal regulators will use a lighter touch with industry. But the core of Trump's promise to "drain the swamp" is the same goal of deregulation that Republicans have sounded for decades.

Looking back at decades of reform promises, there was little in the way of an overarching theory to galvanize public support in the way that, say, the rights revolution did in the 1960s, or the progressive movement did at the turn of the last century. Efforts at reform in recent decades focused on specific rigidities, and were not more broadly aimed at, say, giving people responsibility to be sensible.

At this point neither political party has any serious proposal to fix Washington. An angry public is presented with cartoon clichés of reforms that can't possibly work. Deregulation promises amputation, but that's not the right cure for mindless bureaucracy; voters want clean air and clean water, safety oversight, and Medicare. That's why deregulation goes nowhere even when Republicans are in control of Congress. Conversely, trying to prune the bureaucratic jungle, as we learned with President Obama, only has marginal impact. The overbearing rules just grow back with renewed density as bureaucrats obsessively clarify each new ambiguity.

Washington needs more than reform of the current system. It needs to make government work. That requires replacing its massive bureaucracy with a simpler structure that relinks real people with public goals. That's why Washington will resist—not only will that put officials on the hot spot, but decades of arcane expertise will go down the drain. History indicates, however, that inertial forces can only keep the lid on broad discontent for so long. Public opinion is boiling. In 2016 voters elected someone who, by background and temperament, was literally inconceivable to the political establishment. Where will voters push the needle next? One thing seems clear: leadership will not come from the existing parties.

6

Unworkable Political Ideologies

"The insistence ... on a 'rationally perfect'
law code ... leads straight to the
omnipotent total state."

—Peter Drucker

Conservatives and liberals have legitimate differences in their world views. Conservatives want government to get out of people's hair. Liberals want government to address long-term needs, including climate change and inequality. I find myself agreeing with conservatives such as Friedrich Hayek on individual initiative, and with liberals like Arthur Schlesinger on the need for stewardship for the future.

Conservative and liberal ideologies on how to govern, on the other hand, are just different versions of correctness. Their common assumption is that restricting official authority enhances freedom—whether through detailed rules or expansive rights. Both liberal and conservative visions of correctness ensure public ineptitude.

The Republican and Democratic parties are usually reviled

for being shortsighted and hypocritical. Indeed, their one predictable trait is irresponsibility: the prudent choice may be right in front of them—say, balancing the budget—but they won't reach for it. Does America need new political parties? Savvy insiders say that's impossible. Sooner or later, they say, partisan awfulness might be overcome by campaign finance reform, and other traditional political means.

But, even with better people, neither party will ever lead a broad overhaul of government. One reason is that virtually all interest groups will oppose cleaning out the stable—they exist to preserve the status quo, and make their living shoveling the muck. No conceivable version of either party is likely to repudiate these interest group alliances. That's why a new party is needed.

A new party is needed also because accepted conservative and liberal ideologies must be repudiated. I doubt that most Democrats or Republicans have really thought through their ideologies. The philosophical tags generally fall into the bin of received wisdom from prior generations. "I'm a libertarian." "I believe in individual rights." Nor do party hacks actually honor these concepts when governing; most decisions seem driven more by interest group demands than by ideological principles.

Ideologies nonetheless are critical because they frame public discussion. That's why party platforms and rhetoric are predictably boring. Year after year, the parties say the same thing: blah, blah, individual rights, blah blah, deregulation. (The attraction of Trump to many is his willingness to deviate from any script, and say just about anything).

The ideologies of both parties are propped up by half-truths. Conservatives are correct, for example, that individual ownership of daily choices is essential to accomplishment. Liberals are correct that government oversight is needed to safeguard common resources and protect against abuses. But their respective ideologies on how to organize public choices assure mutual deadlock and the slow suffocation of the rest of society.

Conservative Ideological Errors

Libertarians. Conservative advocacy for individual freedom, especially in daily choices, is grounded in the effectiveness of market forces to allocate goods effectively and stimulate greater prosperity. The focus on free markets is commonly associated with the libertarian branch of conservatism.

Hard-core libertarians go further, however, and embrace markets almost as a theology. Thus, in the aftermath of Hurricane Harvey, which struck Houston in 2017, one commentator argued that price gouging was the best way to allocate scarce water supplies. Let the rich people buy water at, say, $50 per bottle, and other vendors will have a powerful incentive to increase water supplies. As an economic analysis, he may have been correct, leaving aside what happens to thirsty people in the lag time before new supplies arrive.

But governing involves values as well as economics. Most people consider price gouging unfair. Letting rich people get first in line for water would offend even our laissez-faire forebears. Hayek specifically used the example of water shortage to explain how market solutions can go too far. But the patron saint for libertarians, Nobel economist Milton Friedman, advocated such solutions with enthusiasm.

Novelist Ayn Rand popularized selfishness as the guiding

principle for libertarians: "Man exists for his own sake, . . . the pursuit of his own happiness is his highest moral purpose." But Americans believe in community, not just atomized self-interest. Tocqueville's formulation of "self-interest rightly understood"—the drive to help the broader society as well as yourself—is far closer to American values than unbridled self-ishness. This requires the capacity to make common choices.

Most libertarians readily acknowledge that markets require the protection of the Rule of Law—for example, to enforce contracts and stop crime. But it's hard to find their vision of how government should make common choices. Libertarians are so interested in stopping government meddling (often correctly) that they can't focus on how government might work better. Who decides what is pollution? Or draws the line on what is a reasonable lawsuit?

Libertarians have no positive philosophy of governing. They have a philosophy of *not* governing. Their guiding precept—individual ownership of choices—embodies a powerful truth about human motivation and the invisible hand of markets. But libertarianism offers little on how government can make practical choices, or can achieve public oversight without suffocating freedom. Radical libertarianism drives over a cliff by preaching selfishness as a social good. Values are the mortar of a healthy society. Contracts rest on norms of good faith and fair dealing. If Ayn Rand had her way, an epidemic of distrust would corrode the very markets that libertarians place such faith in.

Conservative Distrust of Authority. Where libertarians focus on free market solutions, other conservatives focus on the flip side of the coin—the perils of state power. Conservatives rightly fear arbitrary authority. The Framers would agree that officials should not have carte blanche to do whatever they want to advance public goals.

But conservatives do not focus on avoiding arbitrary authority; they want to minimize almost all state authority. The "first duty [of] public officials," Barry Goldwater wrote in *Conscience of a Conservative*, "is to divest themselves of the power they have been given." According to conservative orthodoxy, authority is a zero-sum game—the less state authority, the more freedom for citizens.

The conservative obsession against authority is almost perfectly counterproductive. Authority is not a zero-sum phenomenon. Authority is the hub where necessary common choices are made. If the teacher lacks authority to maintain order, students can't learn. Unless officials have authority to make a timely decision, permits for new business or infrastructure get bogged down in bureaucracy. A crowded society needs traffic cops; otherwise we get stuck in gridlock. Without authority, conservative values also lose their mechanism for action. Conservatives after the 1950s became " 'obsessed with liberty,' " historian Eric Foner observes, when prior conservative leaders thought "they ought to be concerned with duty, responsibility, and moral order."

Trying to avoid arbitrary authority with detailed dictates results, ironically, in giving officials arbitrary authority. No citizen or business, not even a corporation with hundreds of lawyers, can comply with dense rulebooks. Any official can readily find infractions. Is your paperwork in order?

Limiting judicial authority is also received wisdom among the right: judges should only apply law, not make law. Conservatives seek to curb the evil of judicial activism—judges

who take it upon themselves to make legislative decisions—
such as Judge Arthur Garrity ordering "busing" in Boston in
the 1970s to achieve racial balance, with disastrous social and
political consequences.

But judicial restraint, like deregulation, is overbroad. Yes,
courts should avoid acting like legislatures, just as Congress
should avoid overbearing regulations. But freedom depends
upon courts drawing lines on who can sue for what, protecting against overreach both by the state and by private litigants.
The job of courts is to protect freedom, not accept at face value
extreme arguments by either side to a lawsuit.

The Tea Party movement sprang up out of frustration with
the inability of anyone, including Republican leaders, to rein in
the excesses of Washington. Disrupting Washington is the goal
of these alternative movements. "Just say no" to government.
Conservative activist Grover Norquist succeeded in getting
virtually all Republican members of Congress to sign a "no new
taxes" pledge.

The flaw in this approach is that it offers no positive vision
of how to govern better. Conservative nihilists throw monkey
wrenches into the gears, with no apparent concern for the moral
implications of, say, running up the federal deficit by refusing to
raise sufficient revenue to pay for Medicare and other federal
services. Indeed, there's a gleeful quality to their nihilism. "I
don't want to abolish government," Norquist quipped, "I simply
want to reduce it to the size where I can drag it into the bath-
room and drown it in the bathtub." Like the hyenas in Disney's
The Lion King who jump up and down at the prospect of "No
king, No king," Tea Party activists have no sense of responsibility for how government should actually function.

Federalism. Federalism is a doctrine of delegating the central power of Washington down to individual states. Let each state decide, for example, how to provide Medicaid. As I discuss below, government generally works better when decisions are close to the ground. The new Mario Cuomo bridge across the Hudson River, replacing the Tappan Zee bridge, was approved and built in record time because Governor Andrew Cuomo plowed through bureaucratic obstacles.

Federalism is hardly a panacea, however. Most states are also paralyzed by dense bureaucracy. Some large states are functionally insolvent, and are in the grips of special interests such as public unions. Delegating responsibility downward won't be effective if the responsible local people don't have the room to achieve sensible results. Federal leverage may be essential to dislodge state intransigence. States can also jump the rails under charismatic leadership, à la George Wallace. Washington may be needed to exercise distant oversight.

———

Bad authority, conservatives correctly observe, is the enemy of freedom. No authority, however, is also the enemy of freedom. The "simultaneous recession of both freedom and authority in the modern world" is no coincidence, Hannah Arendt observed. In an interdependent society, a hierarchy of authority empowers everyone in the chain. What good are your ideas if the official lacks the authority to act on them?

The thread running through all these conservative ideologies, including federalism, is that Republicans don't actually want to govern. Sitting up in the peanut gallery, Republicans attack the regulatory state but refuse to take responsibility for making the hard choices needed to fix it. Are they the party for overhauling government?

Liberal Ideological Failures

The newish century presents many new challenges for government. Global markets can destroy the employment base of a town overnight. Main Street has been smashed by the double whammy of big box stores and online retail. Technological and logistical superiority creates natural monopolies that overwhelm markets and commoditize jobs, keeping wages low and reducing opportunities for personal advancement. Pollution travels across borders, and oceans are overfished.

Unlike conservatives, who assume the market can take care of these things, liberals correctly see these modern phenomena as requiring state intervention. But the solutions are far from obvious. That's why it's hard to find concrete reforms from liberals. Raise the minimum wage to $15, Bernie Sanders proposed. But that just drives jobs overseas or hastens the substitution of robots. Probably better to expand the "earned income tax credit," where government provides a supplemental payment to get workers up to a living income. But that too might have unintended consequences. Fixing the economic and social ills identified by liberals will require local innovation as well as central stimulus, engaging the will and creativity of citizens on the ground. This requires a governing philosophy that empowers people, not red tape reaching into the heartland from Washington.

Liberals want government to do more, but today it's hard to find liberal leaders like Jimmy Carter and Al Gore who focus on how government actually does things. Reading through liberal critiques of modern society, I am struck by the absence of any coherent governing vision. For example, economist Joseph Stiglitz, a Nobel laureate, in *The Price of Inequality* addresses various failings of society such as income disparity and failing schools. But he assumes throughout that the flaw is lack of adequate funding, and pays little attention to unmanageable bureaucracy.

Democrats have their heads in the sand about the failures of Washington. Environmental review should be preserved as is, liberals argue, even if it (1) is thousands of pages long, (2) is unintelligible to any citizen, (3) prolongs polluting bottlenecks for years, and (4) doubles the effective cost of needed infrastructure—because, well, every liberal knows that environmental review is good. It also gives a veto to environmental groups who, last I looked, were not elected to make those decisions.

In the 2016 election, Hillary Clinton had no meaningful agenda to address voter frustration with Washington. The Democratic platform is almost completely devoid of any ideas on how to make government more responsive and less wasteful. More government is the theme: More rights! More regulation! More money!

Democrats fantasize about the virtue of public goals while ignoring the reality of public failure and selfishness. Democrats have a two-pronged formula to guarantee continued public failure: never admit current programs are failing, and insist upon rights-based decisions that preclude practical choices.

Individual Rights Against Whom? No concept is more sacred to liberals than individual rights. With most governing decisions, liberals look to how a decision might affect an individual or subgroup. The microscope focuses on whoever is complaining, and asks, "Could anything be done to help or to alleviate the hardship?"

Fairness is important, of course, but fairness to whom? Honoring the "right" of an emotionally disturbed student to be mainstreamed in the classroom may cause disruptions of the learning of all other students. The civil rights movement rightly objected to laws forcing one group to sit in the back of the bus. But civil rights leaders did not suggest that the order be switched. Giving a preference to disabled students, or unilateral power to environmental groups, is a sure formula for resentment.

A problem with "identity politics," as liberal professor Mark Lilla explains, is that it flips public priorities away from issues affecting the common good. Most Americans want good jobs and good roads, and are less attracted to political leaders committed to crusading for the rights of every self-identified subgroup. To attract moderates, Democrats need to help everyone, not just a long list of the disadvantaged.

Looking at public choices through the lens of individual rights is a formula for paralysis. Every public choice hurts somebody. Governing always requires balance and trade-offs. A new drug may save the lives of thousands, but have adverse side effects for a small subgroup. Delaying that decision will kill people. Individual rights is incoherent as a governing philosophy because it doesn't acknowledge everyone's else's rights. Society can't be run by the lowest common denominator.

The constitutional concepts of individual rights and due process were meant to be shields against state coercion, not swords to get advantages over other free citizens. They need to be put back on the constitutional altar, and not used for selfish ends. The liberal reform vision also includes reform of the electoral process. Campaign funding is sleazy, and diverts elected officials from the job of governing, consuming up to half their time. Gerrymandering to create "safe seats" is also pernicious; in a conservative district, for example, there's no incentive for officials to take moderate positions. Almost any disruption of the campaign rules, in my view, will be useful.

But liberals think electoral purity is all that's needed. Just get rid of those party hacks, and democracy will finally work. But new people won't do much without a new vision. Once Congress is filled with 535 acolytes of Mother Teresa, how will they fix things? What's their idea on how to make schools work better, or control health-care costs? Other than spending more money, liberals have no clearer idea of how to fix things than Donald Trump does. I'm all for better people, but there's still a need for a new governing philosophy. You can't govern merely by riding a high horse waving a sword against injustice.

———

Government can never work with an intrusive legal microstructure that prevents officials from making practical choices. Nor can Republicans relieve the burden of overbearing government with a deregulation agenda that's all or nothing; the last four Republican presidents have achieved, basically, nothing on that front. Democrats can never free up resources for climate change and income inequality by demanding ever more entitlements and defending heavy regulatory burdens with marginal benefits. Peter Drucker saw it coming. Striving for a "perfect law code" can only lead to a central state that is "big rather than strong; . . . fat and flabby rather than powerful; . . . costs a great deal but does not achieve much." Drucker blamed the rationalist obsession of both liberals and conservatives. "The rationalist liberal sees his function in the opposition to the injustices, superstitions and prejudices of his time . . . to him the good is only the absence of evil." As to conservatives: "Just to sweep away something— however bad—is no solution. . . . Unless a functioning institution is put into the place of the destroyed institution, the ensuing collapse . . . will breed evils which may be even worse."

"Ultimately we will need a new political theory," Drucker concluded, to overcome "the actual lack of control" by a state tangled in red tape. Where is that new theory? I don't see anything resembling a practical approach to governing by political leaders, nor any partisan appetite for a new governing philosophy. They are professional phonies, indifferent to the realities underlying public failures.

My view is to let the parties marginalize themselves. Let the Republican Party shrivel into a fringe group of right wing anarchists. Let the Democratic Party shrivel into a fringe group promising utopia while doing the bidding of public unions and trial lawyers.

Americans who want a practical society should come together behind a new party, perhaps called the Practical Party. Initially it might be a subparty or movement, available to politicians from both sides, as the Progressive movement was. It could wield power by forming a voting bloc in the center. The governing philosophy of the new party, as Drucker suggested, should be to empower "the individual to be able to make decisions that get the right things done."

PART II

FOUR PRINCIPLES FOR PRACTICAL GOVERNMENT

A PRACTICAL GOVERNMENT REQUIRES ALLOCATing responsibility for who does what. It also requires opening doors to choices that today are barred as subjective—about practical trade-offs, about people's character, and about ultimate values of right and wrong. Simplifying the governing framework is one step to empowering people at the point of implementation. Equally important, but harder, is creating a new vocabulary and culture of governing. We need to relearn how to take responsibility.

I've identified four organizational choices that have been banished by correctness and are essential for public decisions that are practical and fair: (1) giving subjective authority to a responsible decision maker; (2) holding people accountable; (3) adapting law to new circumstances; and (4) asserting moral values. Empowering people to take responsibility to make these choices requires, in each case, new structures and beliefs that contravene current assumptions. I now discuss each in order.

7

Give Responsibility to Identifiable People

"Responsibility, to be effective, must be individual
responsibility.... As everybody's property in effect
is nobody's property, so everybody's responsibility
is nobody's responsibility."

—Friedrich Hayek

Nothing will get done sensibly, as discussed, unless a person or small group of people can take responsibility to make it happen. This is not a point of view, or an ideology, but a truth. Human responsibility is the oxygen of accomplishment. This is as valid in government as in any other activity. Projects succeed because people focus on the goal, and get there by taking risks, adapting, innovating, making do, and learning from failure.

Responsibility is a powerful motivator: it embodies both reward and risk, and it provides meaning and self-respect by allowing people to do things in their own way. Any organization needs "a principle of management," Peter Drucker concluded, "that will give full scope to individual strength and responsibility." Management theories and structures succeed only as tools of responsibility, not replacements.

Making people take responsibility for actual results does not seem radical. That's how life works everywhere else. But achieving this vision requires a complete overhaul of Washington and, eventually, most state governments as well. That's because responsibility requires a measure of authority. The extent of authority will be constrained by law, and safeguarded by oversight up a hierarchy, but authority means that the official can make "particular decisions without having to ask someone else's permission."

Instead of a legal labyrinth, the spotlight would shine on an identifiable official. Things go wrong; some public employee stands up and tries to fix it; if that doesn't work out, that official or another one explains why and tries something else. Citizens must see action, effect, and further action. There's someone to blame, or praise. There are concrete choices that a political candidate can vow to change, or support. Only then will we feel our views and votes matter.

Responsibility in a democracy puts the focus of public policy where it should be—evaluating the performance of the official, not the demands of private claimants. The civil servant's job is to serve the common good. Today, the inversion of authority puts the focus on whoever is complaining. Tomorrow, the responsible official must instead frame the decision as what is fair and sensible for society.

Washington today is a black box. That's another reason so many Americans are apathetic. Why bother? The absence of a lever to influence government not only contributes to apathy, but also to its evil twin, extremism. When yelling at a black box, rhetoric has nowhere to go but up. Rebuilding a hierarchy of responsible officials will get democracy working again. Giving officials the authority to take responsibility, however, requires overcoming a number of hurdles. The first is that many, perhaps most, officials in Washington will do almost anything to avoid it.

Fear of Responsibility

In 2015, following publication of the Common Good report "Two Years, Not Ten Years," I was summoned to the White House to discuss with senior officials their efforts to streamline infrastructure approvals. They told me that a recent law (misnamed the FAST Act) would resolve most of the delays. The FAST Act created a new sixteen-agency council to resolve interagency disputes, and provided twenty pages of new procedures (on top of all the existing procedures) for how this new interagency council would work. The FAST Act included this model of circularity as its ultimate provision to resolve disputes: "If a dispute remains unresolved . . . the Director of the Office of Management and Budget . . . shall . . . direct the agencies party to the dispute to resolve the dispute."

I had a few questions. "How long will it take to schedule a meeting with sixteen busy officials?" They didn't know. "How much authority will each attendee have to compromise his agency's position?" Again, no idea. "Just in case the attendees don't agree," I finally asked, "who has authority to make a decision?" The senior official quickly responded: "Oh, no one has that authority. That would be too dangerous."

Correctness has cowed America's entire public culture. Any reform discussion quickly gets bogged down in process talk on how to get to a decision without any identifiable official having to decide. The one taboo is giving anyone that authority.

What accounts for this obsessive avoidance of human responsibility? One explanation is fear. "Liberty means responsibility," George Bernard Shaw observed: "That is why most men dread it." Responsibility is especially frightening when people are surrounded by failure, and feel buffeted by forces beyond their control. People will prefer the security of an authoritarian system to freedom, as psychoanalyst Eric Fromm explained in *Escape from Freedom.*

An irony of bureaucratic culture is that the less accountable officials are, the more they fear taking responsibility. Charlie Peters, the founder of *The Washington Monthly*, described this "near-total preoccupation with self-protection. . . . It is ironic that a system intended to protect the courageous and outspoken has attracted people who . . . are looking for protection against anything that could disturb their quiet but steady progress up the career ladder."

Most officials probably don't think they're avoiding responsibility. To them, responsibility means complying with all the rules and procedures. They go to meetings, talk in bureaucratic tongues, and sometimes, after years, something happens. This is the professional culture of Washington—so deep in the bureaucratic rut that there's no line of sight to public purpose. Actual decisions seem almost like accidents.

Cultures are hard to change. Max Weber said that bureaucracies, once entrenched, are permanent: "the resulting system

...is practically indestructible." Within the machinery of Washington, people can't imagine doing things differently.

Avoidance of responsibility extends to elected leaders as well. When Senator Dale Bumpers retired, he observed that members of Congress "want to be elected, but we don't want to govern." Democratic congressman Jim Cooper says that his colleagues talk about reform, but don't want to be "responsible for proposals they have defended on television, bragged on in speeches, and received major contributions for pushing."

Avoiding responsibility is also a disease of special interests. Business lobbyists insist on what they call "clear law" to supplant any decision-making authority. Whatever government does, they insist, must be implemented according to specific rules laid out in advance. That's why the Volcker Rule, designed to avoid proprietary trading by banks, ballooned to 950 pages. Paul Volcker himself thought it could have been done in a few pages.

Washington is a city of agents acting on behalf of clients and the public, not striving for self-directed goals. Agents tend to worry first about avoiding blame, not getting to a result. We imagine that special interests are using their influence to get favors, but mainly the lawyers and lobbyists that represent them cling to the status quo. Reform is too risky.

During Al Gore's reinventing government initiative, I had made headway with congressional leaders with a regulatory simplification proposal, where business and regulators would both have more flexibility to work out the best regulatory solutions. Then the proposal was killed by big business lobbyists, who insisted on detailed rules set out in advance. A month later

I was seated next to the CEO of a large chemical company at a lunch hosted by Vice-President Gore, and I asked him what he would think of a flexible regulatory program. "I would take that in a second," he said. "Often the regulations don't serve any-one's interests. I'd welcome the ability to sit down with the regulator and work out what makes sense."

Citizens too have enjoyed a kind of vacation from democratic responsibility. When the rules of correctness tell everyone exactly what to do, citizens don't need to worry about whether officials are doing a good job. Even now, when the rules are driving Americans nuts, our instinct is that Washington should produce better rules. Our fifty-year vacation from active democracy has to come to an end. When officials have authority to make decisions, that will put pressure on us to be vigilant. No more reclining in the Barcalounger and griping at the television.

Democracy can't work as an automatic system of uniform controls. Philosopher John Plamenatz explained that the great thinkers about democracy, including Alexander Humboldt, John Stuart Mill, and Tocqueville, "feared paternal government no less than oppression by the state. If the state looks after the citizen too well . . . it weakens his self-reliance and independence of judgment, his ability to define his own problems and to set about solving them. Freedom is the school of freedom." Only with freedom can people learn to take responsibility, including overseeing decisions by others.

America's programmed public culture must be disrupted. This requires new officials, in new locations and a culture of accountability, as I will shortly discuss. Fear of taking responsibility can only be overcome by greater fear of something else. Fear of what? Fear of your boss and co-workers. Fear of failure. Fear of public opinion. Fear of authority, as Hobbes reminded us, is an essential element of a working society. Officials must not have the option of avoiding responsibility. Citizens too must fear what happens if they don't pay more attention.

An entirely new, and radically simpler, legal code is required to create an open framework that requires fresh decisions at every level of responsibility. That new legal framework will put the spotlight on particular officials, not sweep back and forth across the surface of the giant black box.

The superstructure of modern bureaucracy that must be disassembled includes not only cultural and organizational assumptions, but also the legal orthodoxy that exalts clear rules over human responsibility. Here is an overview of why the myths of current legal philosophy should be repudiated without regret.

Restoring a Human Rule of Law

Every law school for fifty years has taught its students that public law is about guaranteeing correctness through detailed rules, individual rights, and due process. Minimizing human authority, legal mandarins have told us, results in a purer form of the Rule of Law. The legitimacy of this correctness philosophy has been unquestioned, with only occasional sparks of dissent, for half a century now. It must be discarded.

Correctness is not a valid goal for law, but its antithesis. Constant legal justification undermines law's main purpose:

protecting our freedom. Think about it: What kind of legal system doesn't let teachers, doctors, officials, and others act sensibly?

Let's go back to first principles. No respected formulation of freedom prevents people from acting responsibly. "The end of law is not to . . . restrain, but to preserve and enlarge freedom," to quote John Locke. Law protects our freedom in two ways. It shields us from state coercion—government can't take our property or liberty except by law. And law also protects us from abuses by other people—they can't cheat, pollute, breach contracts, and so forth. By covering our backs, law liberates us to marshal our energies towards achieving our own goals.

Correctness, on the other hand, focuses only on eliminating abuses. It does so by removing our freedom. "In their zeal to create social and economic conditions" for better freedom, Isaiah Berlin noted, reformers "tend to forget freedom itself." Instead of striding towards our goals, we tiptoe through the day, constantly looking over our shoulders to guard against claims of legal incorrectness. Have you followed all the rules? Are you sure? Might that comment be taken the wrong way?

The error is not just a matter of degree—not just, for example, an inevitable cost of the growth in the scope of government oversight. The error is conceptual: correctness basically inverts law and freedom, in each of the following ways:

Law is not supposed to define what's reasonable—there are many ways to be reasonable—but to define and protect against what's unreasonable. Law is a concept of outer boundaries, as noted earlier, like a fence around a broad field. The fence defines the boundaries of freedom by drawing the line on unreasonable behavior. Within those legal boundaries is a broad field of freedom in which people are free to do whatever they want, however they want to do it. Law sets "frontiers, not artificially drawn," as Isaiah Berlin put it, "within which men should be inviolable." Law stands on the edges of the field, like a policeman standing guard against conduct that crosses the line. Law's inquiry is intrinsically negative: Was the person driving carelessly? Was the decision an abuse of discretion?

Correctness, by contrast, imposes affirmative plans on how to do things properly: Correctness is a nanny striving for human perfection throughout society. Instead of guarding outer boundaries, correctness intercedes in every daily interaction where something *might* go wrong. Correctness thus represents a huge expansion of state power—like, say, telling us how to cook instead of protecting against adulterated ingredients.

There is no such thing as "clear law" that can define correct behavior. Correctness is propped up by muddled thinking over the way law works. Even brilliant thinkers on human freedom fall into the trap of thinking that public choices fall into only two categories: either (1) clear law that is implemented objectively, like a speed limit, or (2) anything goes, with no constraints on official discretion.

Because "clear law" produces thick rulebooks that are unintelligible to real humans, one would have thought that sensible people would question this myth of clarity. Moreover, deciding what is bad behavior always requires a measure of human judgment. "Justice ... is a concept by far more subtle and indefinite," Justice Benjamin Cardozo observed, "than any that is yielded by mere obedience to a rule." Enforcing the boundaries of law requires judges and officials to draw on accepted norms of reasonableness.

Let's take a simple situation. Most sensible people probably agree that it's unfair, as required under "zero tolerance" rules, to suspend a first grader because he brought to school a toy soldier carrying his toy rifle. On the other hand, a high school student who brings a switchblade should be immediately suspended. School principals can discern these differences. That's why, as noted earlier with immigration policy, zero tolerance rules are absurd; principals need the authority to make sensible disciplinary decisions. If we're worried about principals who lack an internal gyroscope to make fair decisions, then we should make it easier to replace bad principals. Instead, in our devotion to "clear law," we compel every principal in America to act like an idiot.

Most choices at the legal boundary will be more nuanced than distinguishing between a tiny plastic soldier and a real switchblade. The more nuanced the choice, however, the more human judgment is required.

Letting judges and officials interpret law does not give them arbitrary power. The mandarins of correctness think that any freedom to use judgment in law—especially by officials—is an invitation to abuse. What they misunderstand is that, by defining a scope of responsibility, law hems in the range of action and creates a hierarchy by which other people hold the official accountable. Our protection against official abuse is not mindless compliance, but oversight by other officials and judges of the first official's fidelity to his legal responsibility.

Every respected legal system relies on humans to interpret it in the particular context. The Constitution, for example, protects your free speech in one phrase that prevents Congress from "abridging the freedom of speech." It's been interpreted by courts in many different contexts, and most of us couldn't define exactly its boundaries. But few people lose sleep over the gray areas at the edges because we trust that its basic norms are widely accepted, including by prosecutors and judges. This one short principle is good enough to inspire confidence that even the president lacks the power to muzzle your criticism.

Until the correctness craze of the past fifty years, law was mainly goals and general principles, meant to be applied with common sense and prevailing norms. American contract law, generally regarded as reliable and predictable, rests on principles such as "commercial reasonableness" and "good faith." Law also needs prescriptive rules—say speed limits or effluent limits—but these work best in settings where rigidity is preferable from a utilitarian standpoint.

Law is a human institution, not an automated program. It avoids abusive enforcement not by mechanical precision but by a hierarchy of oversight and accountability. Separation of powers is a concept that presumes that each of the separated powers is led by humans—real people—whose scope of responsibility is to provide oversight by their independent judgment.

Looking at the boundaries of law under a microscope, what you should see is a cellular construction where each official has defined jurisdiction, with outer boundaries, similar to the framework of freedom itself. Surrounding that official are other officials and judges with independent powers to overturn any rogue decisions.

Law based on general principles has the virtue of affirming norms of right and wrong. Decisions can be practical and fair, instead of brittle and ineffective. Another virtue of a simple, open framework defining a scope of responsibility is that it *requires* officials to be sensible and fair. Officials are not only free to do what's right, but are on the hook if they do not.

We respect the current system because it's impartial and authorized by democracy. Democracy is not the same as freedom, however. As Tocqueville put it, "For myself, when I feel the hand of power lie heavy on my brow, I care but little to know who oppresses me; and I am not the more disposed to pass beneath the yoke because it is held out to me by the arms of a million men." The angry Americans described in *Hillbilly Elegy* and showing up in rallies for Trump seem to feel the same heavy hand upon their brow, and are not mollified by the fact that Washington is acting lawfully.

The test of law is how it works. That's why the current legal philosophy, which undermines our freedom to do what's right and sensible, must be abandoned.

New Codes Should Allocate Responsibility To Meet Goals

Writing a new code that restores responsibility is not a vast drafting exercise because there's no need to struggle over details of implementation. Australia in the 1980s replaced thick rulebooks for nursing homes with thirty-one general principles—for example, to provide a "homelike environment." Within a short period, nursing homes were markedly better, because, as researchers John and Valerie Braithwaite found, the operators, regulators, and family representatives started focusing on quality instead of compliance.

New codes should aim at giving official and citizens the responsibility to achieve public goals in their own ways. People can try different ideas and adapt when things don't work out. In Australia, the uncertainties of what would work best meant that stakeholders had an incentive to cooperate and compromise. Issues were worked out in conferences with owners, staff, residents, and relatives.

Common Good, the nonpartisan reform group that I chair, has a legislative proposal to streamline infrastructure red tape that is not quite three pages long—basically allocating responsibility to designated officials to make and oversee needed decisions. Under the proposal, the chair of the Council on Environmental Quality—the White House office created by Congress to oversee environmental review—would have the responsibility to resolve disputes over the scope and adequacy of environmental review. The CEQ chair would still be obligated to meet the goals of the underlying statute, and could not slough off the need for environmental review. No longer would vital infrastructure projects be delayed for years, however, to prepare thick reports with thin benefits—such as reports on historic buildings on a project that impacts no buildings.

Humans taking responsibility, not rules, are the main variable for achieving high quality in hospitals, nursing homes, and day-care centers. Safety too is mainly about training and oversight, not better equipment. Many of the 4,000 detailed rules in the federal worker safety law could be replaced by this principle: "Tools and equipment should be reasonably suited for the use intended, in accord with industry standards." General principles leave room for argument at the margins, but, as noted, those discussions tend to promote sensible decisions.

Regulatory judgment is vital for safety because of unavoidable trade-offs. Safety is only half an idea; the question is what we're giving up to be safe. Guidelines discouraging children from running around and exploring on their own are counterproductive. It's hard to be streetwise unless you've been allowed on the street. The seminal essay here is Aaron Wildavsky's *The Secret of Safety Lies in Danger*, which explains why caution often increases risk.

The future is unknown; this too is a reason it's a mistake to plan with much detail. "No plan," a general once said, "survives contact with the enemy." No detailed regulation survives contact with the facts. That's why people must have responsibility to meet public goals. Not all people will succeed in their responsibility, of course. Some officials will be ham-fisted and unreasonable, just as some citizens will be careless or delusive. Judgments about people are critical for managing government institutions. That's why the second essential choice for a practical society is to restore the ability to hold officials accountable.

8

Restore Accountability to Public Culture

"How can one expect rational administration
when good men are held in the same
esteem as bad ones?"

—Polybius

Government works through people. An effective school requires good teachers and an effective principal to lead them. Giving permits on a timely basis requires officials who strive to be helpful. That's why we need these public employees to take responsibility.

But they must be accountable. Without accountability, responsibility will never be given, and will revert immediately to thick rulebooks. Few of us will give power to another without assurance that the person will be accountable if they abuse it. "When men are allowed to act as they see fit," Friedrich Hayek noted, "they must also be held responsible for the results of their efforts."

Accountability has been muddled beyond recognition by the legal conventions of correctness. How do you prove by objective facts that someone has bad judgment, or doesn't try hard, or bores students? Accountability, like responsibility, hinges on judgment. Just as people taking responsibility must be able to draw on their instincts and experience to get the job done, so too co-workers must be able to draw on their instincts about who's doing a good job.

There's nothing radical about what I just said. It's probably how every successful human organization has worked since the beginning of civilization. Accountability is what's required to give people ownership of choices so they can be practical and fair. But restoring accountability to America's public sector will require toppling a huge fortress erected by public unions over the past fifty years, and replacing it with the hierarchy of accountability based on human judgment.

Accountability in the public sector in America is basically nonexistent. This is no secret. More federal employees die on the job than are terminated or demoted. In California, an average of only two out of approximately 277,000 teachers are dismissed for poor performance each year. It's odd, with that perfect pool of good teachers, that California schools are ranked near the bottom among all states.

Unaccountability in government is the result of layers of civil service protections, union contracts, and judicial rulings. The cumulative protections are considered virtually impregnable. That's why school reformers have thrown up their hands, and channeled their energy into charter schools.

Most people think of accountability as firing people. Terminating bad teachers would indeed improve things. Just "replacing the bottom 8 percent of teachers with an average teacher," Stanford professor Eric Hanushek estimates, "would bring the U.S. up to the level of [world-leading] Finland."

Other than wanting to get rid of bad workers, however, most reformers don't think much about overhauling the public personnel system. While reformers consider the hidebound system of rules and union contracts to be regrettable, they think it's a second- or third-level concern—just another in a long litany of public ineptitudes.

Accountability, to the contrary, holds the key to good government. Every virtue we seek in public institutions—public purpose, responsiveness, energy, effectiveness, adaptability, fairness, to name a few—hinges on accountability. Accountability is required for officials to be given responsibility, is essential for shared trust needed to foster energetic public cultures, and is the lever to re-empower democratic governance. Accountability is foundational.

A healthy democracy is impossible with a rotten public culture at the heart of it. To fix American democracy, the sick culture within our governing institutions must be completely rebuilt. Civil service must be reconceived as a genuine "merit system." The role of public unions must be rethought against the ultimate goal of a healthy public culture. The links in the chain of human responsibility and accountability must be reconnected. Public service must become important again, not a sinecure without opportunity or honor.

The Secret to Successful Institutions

In the age of individual rights, almost no one talks about protecting the rights of institutions. Policy makers assume that institutions are the enemy of individuals in a free society, and rarely question the elaborate legal structures erected over the past fifty years to protect individuals against institutional judgments. Public agencies are a favorite target, and at this point are mummified under layers of red tape.

Only a few observers, notably Peter Drucker and sociologist Robert Bellah, have made the critical connection that institutional freedom is essential for individual freedom. The single-minded focus on protecting individuals against institutional judgments has had the paradoxical effect of reducing individual freedom, especially among the workers within the institutions.

The scope of a citizen's freedom in a modern society hinges in large part on public and private institutions. At the broadest level, we rely upon schools, hospitals, social service organizations, regulatory agencies, and businesses to provide essential services and products. These institutions keep our water pure and food safe, and care for us when we're sick. How well they do their job depends in part on whether they are able to respond to our particular needs and ideas. Making institutions work better helps everyone.

Institutions can't achieve their goals and support a free society unless the people within them are free to make the judgments within the scope of their responsibility, including internal institutional decisions. Coordination and cooperation require constant management choices. The concentric rings of responsibility require freedom at each level.

The effect of these institutional choices is not only better schools, hospitals, and agencies but, contrary to the orthodoxy about individual rights, better freedom for employees *within* an institution. Institutions are an expression of their employees, not "objective mechanisms," Bellah observes, "separate from the lives of the individuals who inhabit them." Institutions are the mechanisms by which individuals "understand our own identity and the identity of others as we seek cooperatively to achieve a decent society." To feel free, people within institutions must be able to act on their instincts of right and wrong.

Liberating internal choices is also critical to building a healthy institutional culture. What makes an organization succeed is not mainly the formal structures but the informal ones. Good organizations rely on cultural norms that inspire cooperation and trust. Successful schools, for example, typically have a culture of camaraderie, caring, and going the extra mile. Teachers feel empowered to do what's right, and aspire to meet or exceed expectations, and expect the same of others.

The personal achievement of each public employee, and his job fulfillment, depend on this institutional culture. A person's "abilities do not exist independent of the environment," management expert Chester Barnard observed. The abilities, attitude, and customs of our co-workers are critical to our own achievement.

Healthy institutions all differ, precisely because people mold them in their own way—as corporate executive Dennis Bakke writes: "The feeling that you are part of a team, a sense of community, the knowledge that what you do has real purpose... [where] people are able to use their individual talents and skills to do something useful." By harnessing individual resourcefulness, these organizations achieve more than organizations where people just show up and do the job. Their advantage is the human spirit: "No one has a greater asset for his business," management pioneer Mary Parker Follett wrote, "than a man's pride in his work."

What both government and public employees need to succeed, more than anything, is an energetic and cooperative
public culture. About 22 million Americans work in the public sector, mainly as cops, teachers, and other municipal jobs.
Whether they succeed depends on their ability to take responsibility and solve challenges before them each day. This in
turn depends upon a culture of shared responsibility, where
people feel a sense of ownership of how the institution works
day to day.

Accountability Builds a Fabric of Trust

There are many ways to build a healthy culture, but there is
one condition that all healthy work cultures must satisfy: people must be accountable to the judgments of those they work
with. What's important is the *availability* of accountability—
not actually firing lots of people, which would be discouraging.

Accountability is needed not only to alleviate fear of unchecked
power, but for a positive reason: the prospect of accountability
creates the conditions for trust. Accountability fosters mutual
trust by ensuring that everyone must do his share.

Having a backdrop of accountability is critical to a healthy
organization. "A social organism of any sort whatever, large or
small, is what it is because each member proceeds to his own
duty," William James noted, "with a trust that the other members will simultaneously do theirs."

We often don't know or trust others who work in our organization. What accountability does is make people *trustworthy*. There's an expectation that co-workers will pull their

share, or else. Against that baseline, cooperative cultures can be nurtured.

By contrast, the leverage of trustworthiness turns negative when everyone knows it doesn't matter what you do. That's why the absence of accountability usually kills a culture. Distrust is reinforced when people expect that others will not try hard. When bad performance has no consequences, it discourages good behavior. It's organizational psychology 101: "When a single individual free rides," as one study found, there is a "precipitous decline in teammate contributions." One "bad apple," another study concluded, "can spoil the barrel."

Accountability is usually the job of the supervisor, often reviewed by a personnel committee or other check against unfairness. Accountability relies largely upon subjective perceptions, including about how a person interacts with co-workers. Relying on objective metrics generally causes worse judgments. Judging teachers by test scores of their students, for example, caused teachers to neglect other goals, say, instilling a joy of learning, and in many instances caused educators to resort to cheating.

Intangible attitudes are critical to success. In one study of workers with the same job responsibility, researchers found a dramatic difference in employee effectiveness depending upon whether the employee considered the work as a "calling" or, alternatively, as a "job." Those who saw their work as a calling went out of their way to be helpful. They thought about the ultimate purpose of the enterprise, not just their job description. They raised the morale of co-workers. Shared values and ways of doing things are important also. "The question of personal compatibility or incompatibility is much more far-reaching in limiting cooperative effort than is recognized," Chester Barnard observed. If people don't row together, for any reason, the institution will suffer.

There are countless reasons why some people work out in a job and others do not, relating to personalities, skills, work habits, and office culture. Those that don't fit in should probably work elsewhere. These perceptions about the attitude and fit of particular people will be clear to supervisors and co-workers, but cannot readily be proved by objective criteria. "Laying aside all exceptions to the rule," Professor Philip Jackson found, "there is typically a lot of truth in the judgments we make of others." For an institution to work, people must be free to make these decisions based on their perceptions rather than objective proof. There's nothing sinister about this. Americans on average change jobs ten times between the ages of twenty and forty. This job mobility, propelled in part by people deciding about each other, increases the odds that people will find a workplace they enjoy.

The modern mind is conditioned to believe that losing a job is a cataclysmic event. Whatever sliver of truth there might be in particular cases, it's not true for most people, particularly those who are good workers and readily land on their feet. What's far more dangerous, and unfair, is to tolerate workers who are not doing the job. The cumulative injustice to co-workers and to the enterprise of retaining inadequate workers is far greater than the odd cases where an exemplary employee is let go.

There's no alternative to a hierarchy of accountability. You are free to take responsibility, then your supervisor is free to take responsibility to judge you, and then his supervisor is free . . . and on up the line. Whether these supervisors are wise or fair will be reflected in the workplace culture, for which they should be accountable. "There have to be people who make decisions or nothing will ever get done," Peter Drucker observed. "There have to be people who are accountable for the organization's mission, its spirit, its performance, its results."

Defending Sloth and Worse

The judgments needed for accountability are basically impossible in American government. Public union leaders say that protecting public employees is "just a matter of due process." But the facts say something different. Public unions exist mainly to block any accountability. As one union official admitted, "I'm here to defend even the worst people." Public unions will spend hundreds of thousands of dollars to defend a bad public employee. Los Angeles spent five years and $3.5 million to fire seven teachers. They succeeded with four, at any average legal cost of almost $1 million each.

Regular stories emerge of employees who cannot be terminated despite outrageous behavior—such as the EPA employee who spent the day surfing porn sites, or the transit employee in Boston who, after five disciplinary warnings, pleaded guilty for beating his pregnant girlfriend with a chain. He was ordered reinstated and awarded $96,844 in back pay; his guilty plea, the arbitrator ruled, did not constitute legal "proof."

In *Tailspin*, Steven Brill describes how legal sophistry works in these cases:

> One hearing that I watched involved a fifth-grade Brooklyn teacher. Her five-thousand-page transcript

for a hearing that ended up stretching over forty-five hearing days revealed that she had failed to correct student work, prepare lesson plans, or fill out report cards. The morning I sat in on the hearing, her union-paid lawyer contested whether there was any proof that the teacher had ever possessed the instruction manual that told her to do all of these basic tasks.

The head of the Veterans Administration hospital in Phoenix, at the center of a 2014 scandal over falsified waiting times, was found not accountable for "lack of oversight" because, as Brill recounts, the government failed to prove specific items of no oversight—overlooking the fact that oversight, by definition, is not limited to specific criteria.

Accountability in the public sector is basically upside down—trying to hold a public employee accountable puts the klieg lights on the supervisor. In this weird world, any negative comment by a supervisor in the personnel file gives rise to a right to file a grievance and demand a legal hearing. That's why, a 2016 GAO report found, over 99 percent of federal civil servants were rated "fully successful" or better.

If an accountability proceeding ever gets to the merits of job performance, the ultimate decision turns not on whether an employee does the job well, but whether he's so much worse than everyone else: "Is this teacher so bad that he should lose his job?" Instead of aspiring to excellence, the legal standard for accountability is a race to the bottom.

In addition to insulating the worst workers from accountability, public unions have also "weaponized" their legal powers to secure dismissals of the best public managers. A 2018 exposé by Kate Taylor in *The New York Times* described how teacher's unions orchestrated scores of anonymous complaints against principals who had successfully turned around failing schools. Their alleged offenses were all in the category of foot faults— for example, serving without official permission as an unpaid director of a nonprofit that raised money for the school. But in a hyperlegalistic system, infractions like these were sufficient to secure removal of the best principals. Their actual sin? They were objects of union ire because they put bad teachers under the spotlight, with the result that the overall performance of their schools had markedly improved.

Creating a Public Culture of Futility

The vacuum of accountability is reflected, not surprisingly, in a listless public culture. Many, perhaps most, government departments are awful places to work. Stories of failing schools and public departments all share a theme of gray futility, with public employees trudging through mindless bureaucracy. Show up at this time; do the appointed work, as slowly as you'd like; talk on the phone with family and friends; leave at five o'clock.

This is the common "institutional neurosis" of bureaucratic offices, as James Scott describes in *Seeing Like a State*, "marked by apathy, withdrawal, and lack of initiative." An appointed official in the Pentagon working in humanitarian relief was surprised when, just as a crisis broke in the Balkans, most of her office just got up and went home. It was five o'clock. A regional head of FEMA went on holiday the day following the 1989

California earthquake because, as he explained, he had nonrefundable plane tickets.

When I was looking at possible reforms of the child welfare agency in Illinois in 2016 and 2017, I was struck by the extent to which officials seemed beat down by the system. They no longer believed they could make a difference. A court-appointed expert panel found a general "absence of responsibility and accountability to ensure that each child receives the services that he/she actually needs."

A 1989 report by the Volcker Commission on civil service found a "quiet crisis" in federal civil service, characterized by "an erosion of performance and morale" and the "inability to recruit and retain a talented work force." Pride had been replaced by resignation. The Commission found that seven of ten federal employees who witnessed fraud, abuse, or waste did not even bother to report what they saw. The second Volcker Commission in 2003 found deep resentment at "the protections provided to those poor performers among them who impede their own work and drag down the reputation of all government workers."

Well-qualified graduates are reluctant to work in these conditions. The Partnership for Public Service, a federal civil service reform group, describes the system as "a relic of a bygone era" that is "serving as a barrier" to attracting skilled public servants.

Accountability has been dead for so long that reformers have given up trying. There's a broad sense that public service is a dead end. Free-market conservatives believe that the public sector is condemned to being sluggish because there are no market forces pushing people to perform. But studies by Professor Edward Deci and others demonstrate that humans are motivated more by challenge, and the ability to solve problems, than by money.

Public service can be stimulating. This is demonstrated by pockets of excellence that exist throughout government. The Centers for Disease Control in Atlanta has an exemplary record of confronting contagious diseases worldwide. Its culture, by no coincidence, is mission-driven and famously cooperative. When Dr. James Curran was charged in the early 1980s with spearheading AIDS research, there was a federal hiring freeze, so he asked for volunteers. Eight hundred CDC employees answered the bell. When the contagious, life-threatening Ebola virus began to endanger entire populations, CDC asked for volunteers to go to West Africa to help contain the disease. Two thousand CDC employees volunteered. This is public service at its most noble, comparable to soldiers volunteering for dangerous missions.

Every day, police, firemen and soldiers put their lives on the line to serve the public. The nature of their jobs requires them to stay focused. Any good public school is filled with teachers and principals who go the extra mile to serve their students. These examples of energetic public service only underscore the transformative potential here. What is surprising is not that government fails, but that it works as well as it does. This is a tribute to dedicated public employees who achieve public goals notwithstanding the miserable cultures they're often stuck in.

What's needed is not reforms around the edges, but a complete refocusing of the public employment structure, away from entitlements and towards what it takes to build a responsive, vigorous public culture. It's been a mistake, I think, to battle the public unions in the halls of Congress and state legislatures. The unions are too focused on preserving entitlements to ever give in. What's needed is to pull the legal rug out from under them. It turns out that their power is an accident of history, and violates basic precepts of merit performance, of democratic governance, and of the president's constitutional power under Article II. Judicial intervention is probably the only realistic way to restore accountability to public service.

How the Worm Got in the Apple

A historical halo hovers over civil service because it replaced the Jacksonian spoils system, in which public jobs were handed out to political hacks. Union officials wrap themselves in the cloak of good government, and attack any accountability as violating sacred norms of pure neutrality. Letting supervisors make supervisory judgments, they argue, would create a "system open to cronyism and subjectivity."

Good government actually requires precisely what unions oppose. Civil service was intended to create better accountability, where officials would be judged based on their merit, not political connections. That's why it was called "the merit system." Until the 1960s, civil servants had no tenure, no union collective bargaining agreements, and no due process protections. Government worked tolerably well, and, while government work was rarely known for excitement, until the 1960s it attracted many of the best and brightest graduates. In his study of forest rangers in the 1950s, Herbert Kaufman observed "profound respect and admiration for the Forest Service."

No epidemic of unfairness prompted all the legal protections and union power that now insulates public employees. Immunity from accountability just got swept in during the 1960s rights revolution, greased by political promises from public unions.

History of public employee accountability. For 170 years following ratification of the Constitution, holding federal employees accountable was considered the president's constitutional prerogative. Otherwise "subordinate executive officers" who rendered "inefficient service" or had "lack of loyalty," the Supreme Court held, could "thwart[] the Executive in the exercise ... of his great responsibility."

The issue of presidential power over personnel came to a head in the very first Congress. In what became known as the "Decision of 1789," Madison successfully argued that "the President should possess alone the power of removal from office," which would create an unbroken "chain of dependence ... the lowest officers, the middle grade, and the highest will depend, as they ought, on the President."

The next development was the spoils system, instituted by Andrew Jackson in 1829. This was actually intended as a good-government reform, bringing populist blood into government by politically accountable leaders. Jackson's goal of "rotation in office" quickly got out of hand, and was transformed into a sinecure for incompetent political supporters. Allocating spoils jobs consumed much of politicians' time, just as campaign fundraising does today. When Abraham Lincoln got smallpox, he reportedly quipped, "Tell all the office seekers to come at once for now I have something I can give to all of them."

The assassination of President James Garfield in 1881 by

a disappointed office seeker finally provided the impetus to replace the spoils system with a professional civil service. Contrary to myth, civil service had nothing to do with job protection. Civil service reform provided for neutral *hiring*, not tenure; jobs would no longer be awarded as spoils. The 1883 Pendleton Act "did not restrict the President's general power to remove employees." This was understood both as a constitutional imperative and also as a clear policy guideline that any merit system must include accountability based on performance. As reformer George William Curtis put it, we should not "seal up incompetency, negligence, insubordination, insolence, and every other mischief in the service, by requiring a virtual trial at law before an unfit or incapable clerk can be removed."

For the next eighty years, until the 1960s, the main constraints on firing federal employees were (1) to guard against politically motivated firings (review by a committee, but no "examination of witnesses, trial, or hearing"); and (2) to limit firing of independent and quasi-judicial officials. Otherwise, the general rule, under still-valid Supreme Court precedent, is that the president has the "illimitable power of removal" for officers "in the executive department."

The idea of collective bargaining by public employees was considered antidemocratic, conflicting with their responsibility to serve the public. "The process of collective bargaining, as usually understood, cannot be transplanted into the public service," FDR said: It "manifests nothing less than an intent on their part to prevent or obstruct the operations of Government until their demands are satisfied. Such action, looking toward the paralysis of Government by those who have sworn to support it, is unthinkable and intolerable."

This presumption against public union bargaining power was upended in the 1960s. As payback for union support in his election, JFK by executive order allowed public unions to engage in collective bargaining. JFK's executive order opened the floodgates in state and local governments. In 1967, New York authorized collective bargaining. In 1968, California followed. There was never any public debate on how public unions would affect government.

Paradoxically, the rise of public unions was an unintended consequence of a crusade to snuff out patronage power, as historian Daniel DiSalvo recounts. Good-government reformers had long sought to replace party bosses with professional civil servants untainted by self-interest. But then the expanded civil service itself became the self-interested political force in state and local government. Instead of party bosses handing out jobs and favors to political allies, to be displaced in the next election reversal, public unions provided funding and votes to supportive candidates. Unions settled into a comfortable pattern of negotiating ever-richer contracts for themselves while securing immunity against accountability. As one prominent union leader put it, "We have the ability, in a sense, to elect our own boss."

The rising power of public unions received little attention because it occurred in the middle of the 1960s rights revolution. Similarly, when expanding due process to public management decisions, the Supreme Court expressed no concern for the public's interest in accountable government, or co-workers' interest in employees who did their share. The Court was wearing the blinders of individual rights—focusing on "the severity of depriving a person of the means of livelihood. . . . While a fired worker may find employment elsewhere, doing so will take some time."

The last nail in the coffin of federal employee accountability was the Civil Service Reform Act of 1978, in which Congress codified both collective bargaining and the right of civil servants to trial-like hearings. Under that statute, the president lost almost all authority over executive branch employees.

Nothing in this history suggests a legitimate reason for protecting public employees against accountability. Civil service was created on the principle of merit. Liberal leaders such as FDR saw clearly how public unions would corrode the common good. The reformers who went along with collective bargaining and due process in the 1960s never thought about the effect on morale in public offices. I doubt if Supreme Court justices thought that due process would protect workers who surfed porn sites all day long, or teachers who didn't even bother to grade tests. There's nothing holding in place this unaccountable fiefdom but inertia, defended by raw union power and political payoffs. Ironically, other than the public, the worst victims are public employees themselves.

Remaking Public Service in America

The original goal of civil service is as valid today as in 1883: hire and retain public employees based on merit, not politics. An effective public service requires, in my view, that it meet three basic criteria: public employees should be able, nonpartisan, and accountable. The current system fails miserably on two of the three, and it's not really nonpartisan either—it is partisan to its own entitlements over the public interest. How inefficient do you think this unmanageable system is? Public employees at all levels of government cost about $2 trillion in salary and benefits. Each 10 percent of inefficiency represents an implicit annual tax of $2,000 per American family.

Almost any framework would be better than the current one, particularly if it avoids the conflict of interest against the common good. The Partnership for Public Service proposes a new template that, among other things, scraps the presumption of lifetime service. Why shouldn't bright young Americans come work in government for a few years, and then go back into the private sector?

Reforms like these would be useful but don't go far enough. America must rebuild public employment from the ground up. Rebuilding an accountable public service is the precondition to empowering officials to build dynamic public cultures where they can make a difference—thereby making public service attractive to top graduates. Fairness is also important to a healthy culture, but can be far better provided with termination review committees that include co-workers, as Toyota does in its American plants. Co-workers know who's doing the job far better than a judge in a hyperlegalistic trial. More efficient public management will also free up resources so that officials and teachers can receive compensation that better reflects their responsibilities.

The elephant in the room, blocking the door, is public union power. It's hard to see how responsibility and honor can be restored to public service as long as public unions retain the power of collective bargaining. Their antisocial track record is now embedded in their character. They like wielding power over the workings of government. America's public service today is basically controlled by union bosses, not elected officials. This is not how democracy is supposed to work.

Union rhetoric about "the rights of public employees" is a smokescreen to avoid the reality that public unions have evolved into an enemy of the common good. That's their goal—to get as much as they can, always at the expense of the public. Just as the spoils system needed to be overthrown so that government could focus on public purpose instead of partisan payoffs, so too the corrosive power of the unions needs to be overthrown.

I see two levers to achieve de-unionization of American government: constitutional arguments and federal spending power.

Federal Civil Service is Unconstitutional. Efforts at civil service reform in Congress have withered in the face of union power and public indifference. But there's a more direct path to achieve success—for the president to repudiate the current civil service as a violation of Article II of the Constitution, which mandates that "the executive power shall be vested in a President...."

The constitutional question is this: did Congress have the power to tell the president that he cannot terminate inept or insubordinate employees? The answer I think is self-evident. Executive power is toothless, James Madison observed, if the president has no practical authority over personnel: "If any power whatsoever is in its nature executive, it is the power of appointing, overseeing, and controlling those who execute the laws."

It's impossible to reconcile the President's "illimitable power" to remove executive branch employees under Article II of the Constitution with Congress's mandate in the Civil Service Reform Act of 1978 imposing collective bargaining and trial-type proceedings. Removing the legislative right to trial-type hearings will also remove the predicate for the Supreme Court due process rulings, which hinged on the fiction that public employees had been given a statutory "property right" in their jobs.

President Trump in 2018 issued three executive orders that began to reduce civil service legal protections. Rebuilding a healthy public culture, however, also requires a credible commitment to public service professionalism. There's a reflexive distrust to President Trump that is understandable. His administration's demand for names of Department of Energy employees who worked on climate change, later disavowed, gives credence to fears of politically motivated firings.

Instead of remaking civil service by presidential fiat, I think the president should appoint a special commission to propose a complete overhaul, consistent with core principles of neutral hiring and avoiding partisan dismissals. The president can then implement these reforms by executive order.

State and Local Unions Have Preempted Democratic Rule. Ending public unions in states lacks the constitutional hook of Article II. But there's no realistic political path to public employee accountability because unions basically control the politicians who oversee them. One approach is to present courts with a new constitutional theory to deal with the fact that the public unions have effectively preempted democracy. Not only have public unions broken the links in the chain of democratic accountability, but they have driven a number of states and municipalities to the brink of insolvency so that they can no longer provide adequate services.

The evidence here includes pension arrangements far richer than for comparable industry jobs, demanded and given without any thought of whether taxpayers could afford them. "Sweetening pension benefits" is an "annual event in Albany," Jim Dwyer of *The New York Times* reported in 2018, "like tapping maple trees for sap in the North Country." "Legislators game the next election by awarding benefits that will cost money for decades, without a thought to having enough money for school supplies a few years from now."

Taxpayers are reeling from the burden. Illinois is functionally bankrupt, with one-quarter of the state budget dedicated to pensions ($111 billion in 2015, including over $100,000 each to 14,000 pensioners). About 28 percent of the general revenues of El Monte, California, are spent on pensions. In Oregon "essential services are slashed." As one Oregon city manager put it, "You get to the point where you can no longer do more with less—you just have to do less with less."

Democracy loses any link with electoral accountability if political leaders, in exchange for union support today, can give away taxpayer revenues in future decades, and make it contractually binding so no future political leader can undo it. The negotiating dynamic is the same as paying someone off. It's more insidious than other political deals because the benefit is in the future, and therefore escapes current voter scrutiny. Private-sector unions, by sharp contrast, must negotiate with corporate managers who are accountable to shareholders and no longer get away with such demands.

Asserting presidential power over federal civil service will stimulate public awareness and debate over the role of public unions more broadly. Public outrage might embolden Congress to use the power of the purse to incentivize states to break the union stranglehold. There's a clear federal interest: why should the federal government pour money into public schools or other social programs that cannot be fixed because of the union stranglehold? State legislators will have a hard time explaining to voters why they turned down billions in federal aid in order to do the bidding of public unions.

Inspiring People within Institutions

Institutions are the main mechanism by which individuals relate to the rest of society. They are the hubs for joint action. They are how we relate to broader society. Institutional vitality is essential for our own sense of self-worth. Theologian Reinhold Niebuhr put it this way: "The community requires liberty as much as does the individual; and the individual requires community more than bourgeois thought comprehended."

Institutions must be free to make choices when, inevitably, some people disagree. This includes internal choices about people. Institutional success is mainly about the people. Institutions can't function effectively without judgments by and about people. Nor can individuals find happiness and fulfillment in a work culture where it doesn't matter what anyone does.

Giving public employees a legal shield against the judgments of co-workers was a colossal blunder of the rights revolution. Public institutions became unmanageable, undermining the conditions for human cooperation throughout society. Instead of a rich tapestry of individuals joining with others to achieve common goals, society became bifurcated, as Patrick Deneen concludes, between "the liberated individual and the controlling state." The authority of the institutions and communities in the middle—i.e., the authority of people with institutional responsibility—got lost in the shuffle. The rights revolution made government more inept and unwittingly suffocated the ability to have fulfilling lives within those institutions.

Your freedom is ultimately contingent upon the freedom of others to judge you. Your job is to make co-workers want to work with you. The basic principle for "contentment within the organization," Hayek observed, is "rewarding a man according to what others think." "How faithfully and intelligently . . . how well he has fitted himself into the whole machinery, must be determined by the opinion of other people."

The stakes are high here. People need to be part of institutions with a human scale where they can make a difference, which Yuval Levin calls the "middle layers of society." Being in a cohort of people committed to the common mission not only restores a sense of balance and stability, but can inspire people to accomplish much more than they could ever do by themselves. Famous examples of inspirational cultures include the Florentine artists in the Renaissance, Tin Pan Alley on Broadway, and Silicon Valley. By contrast, institutions and communities where people are preoccupied with personal entitlements are doomed to legalistic controls by the central state, and its downward spiral of misery and alienation.

The threshold question for a functioning institution is whether its leaders are empowered to take responsible actions.

The next question for most organizations is whether the institution is succeeding. If not, the solution usually involves changing some people. People judging people is the currency of successful organizations.

"The true test of a good government," Alexander Hamilton wrote in *Federalist* No. 68, "is its aptitude and tendency to produce a good administration." What would you do about America's public service? I propose a framework where public employees can take responsibility, and where public managers can use the lever of accountability to build a culture of excellence. People who work together well will achieve wonders. We know that's true with sports teams. It's no less true with departments of government.

9
Governing Institutions Must Govern

"The infirmities most besetting popular
governments . . . are found to be defective laws,
which do mischief before they can be mended, and
laws passed under transient impulses, of which
time and reflection call for a change."

—James Madison

Public policy must aspire to be practical, just as officials should be. Programs that are no longer needed should be repealed. Programs that don't work as intended should be amended.

Congress has the responsibility of overseeing laws, but doesn't do its job. Programs and regulations have piled up, decade after decade, with no serious effort to coordinate and cull them. Small businesses, doctors, and teachers trudge through knee-deep requirements, some important, some not. Public resources are wasted in programs that everyone knows are obsolete. Congress is a failed institution for many reasons, but among them is that it doesn't keep law aligned with the needs of society.

Courts work better, and provide impartial forums to resolve · disputes. But courts too must be sensitive to the actual social impact of their rulings. Courts have defaulted almost completely in overseeing how their norms of justice affect the functioning of society. An epidemic of defensiveness has spread across the land. Businesses are scared to give references; teachers won't put an arm around a crying child; disclaimers and warning labels litter our lives—for one reason: lawsuits have no knowable boundaries because courts let people sue for almost anything.

I don't blame Congress and the courts for not fixing the philosophy of correctness. Once that train got going, propelled by guilt and distrust, it is hard to see how anyone could stop it without a countermovement armed with the facts linking correctness to the public's frustrations. But neither Congress nor the courts have even tried to account for the social wreckage left behind by their laws and rulings over the past fifty years. What matters is how law actually works. That's their responsibility.

The Abdication by Congress

A nation of obsolete laws. Congress treats old statutes as immutable features of nature, like a mountain range, rather than mandates from a prior generation that may not meet the needs of America today. The statutory accretion has resulted in a progressive public paralysis, enormous waste, and a cornucopia of unintended results.

Americans constantly find themselves tripped up by laws that make no sense to anyone. For example, a 264-foot fishing trawler was built in 2018 for an American company by the Dakota Creek shipyard in Anacortes, Washington. The state-of-the-art trawler is cleaner, more fuel-efficient, and safer for the rough waters off Alaska than the forty-year-old trawlers currently used by the owner. But about 10 percent of the steel was prefabricated in the Netherlands, which means that the trawler doesn't qualify as American-built under an obscure provision of the 1920 Jones Act, which requires American-made ships for domestic shipping. The owner thus cannot use a safer and cleaner ship made in an American shipyard because of an obscure requirement in a law enacted a hundred years ago—long before global commerce made foreign components almost unavoidable in complex products. The ship might have to be sold to a foreign buyer.

It's hard to find a statutory program that isn't broken. The question is whether it's broken 25 percent or 90 percent. The mandate by Congress in 1975 to provide special education services was not intended to consume 25 percent of total K-12 budgets. That's about $150 billion a year, much more than needed in a less bureaucratic program.

Congress is like the Roach Motel; laws check in but they don't check out. Farm subsidies from the New Deal cost about $15 billion annually; the Davis-Bacon law from 1930, a union freebie that sets wages on federally funded construction projects, raises labor costs by about 20 percent. The 1920 Jones Act, referred to above, doubled the costs of relief shipments to Puerto Rico after Hurricane Maria in 2017.

What is called "the law of the land," Democratic congressman Jim Cooper told me, is "huge piles of laws that are duplicative and ineffective." Cooper pointed to a study of federal job training programs by former Sen. Tom Coburn, which concluded that none of them is effective and had seldom even been studied. Each layer in the "sedimentary process of legislation," Cooper said, was driven by a candidate's desire to "brag about 'creating jobs.' "

Congress's lack of discipline is breathtaking. David Fahrenthold of *The Washington Post* has written a series of articles that resemble comedy more than reality. Try to figure out, for example, whether you are a "small business." There are more than a dozen different definitions. Or what constitutes "Made in USA." The FTC guidance is thirty-seven pages long. Peter Schuck's book *Why Government Fails So Often* contains an inventory of duplicative and counterproductive programs, such as 53 separate programs to spur entrepreneurship, 209 to promote science and math education, and an organ replacement program so bureaucratic that its loss ratio for kidney transplants is double what it should be.

Republicans constantly attack what they view, often correctly, as the unnecessary burden of administrative regulations. Their proposed REINS (Regulations from the Executive in Need of Scrutiny) Act, for example, would prevent any major new rule unless Congress approved it. But this high hurdle for new regulations would do nothing to relieve the burden of existing regulations. Fifty years of regulatory accretion, not next year's stratum of new rules, is what Americans need relief from. Moreover, REINS addresses only agency regulations, and assumes no responsibility for the junkheap of statutes that authorizes all those regulations. Why don't Republicans in Congress clean out their statutory stable first?

Other countries show more discipline. Germany, for example, evaluates the regulatory impact of laws, and adjusts them accordingly. As Chancellor Angela Merkel put it:

Laws are not made for the statute books. They must be made for real life.... This means that law-makers must frame laws in comprehensible language, design them to achieve their intended purpose, and regulate only what really has to be regulated.

The UK's worker safety framework, by contrast to America's, is results-oriented, flexible, and cost-effective. The Organisation for Economic Co-operation and Development (OECD) evaluates the effectiveness of economy-wide regulation of its thirty-six member nations. The United States ranks fifth from last.

Tolerating wasteful and broken programs should be a scandal. I did a rough list of ten wasteful statutory programs and came up with unnecessary costs of almost $1 trillion per year. (My complete list is in the endnotes). This waste, totaling almost $10,000 for each American family each year, doesn't include the burden and frustration of complying with needless regulatory dictates.

Every public dollar involves a moral choice. A dollar spent on a farm subsidy is a dollar not available for, say, modernizing infrastructure. Not facing up to the unavoidable reality of scarcity is an abdication of Congress's core responsibility.

Create One-Stop Shops for Citizens

Most regulations address real needs. An interdependent society, characterized by dealings with people you don't know or trust, creates public demand for government oversight of safe products, competent care, and clean water. But "more is different," as a scientist once observed. More medicine can harm you. More regulatory protections, unless implemented in a practical way, can crush people under unknowable burdens.

Americans think they're regulated by "the government." But in fact they're effectively regulated by multiple governments, as with Indian Ladder Farms, the apple orchard described earlier. Different agencies operate in separate silos, and, among their thousands of requirements, many seem like solutions in search of a problem.

The patriarch of Indian Ladder Farms, Peter Ten Eyck, seventy-nine, thinks that pages of worker safety rules on how to use ladders, or the food safety rule to cover apples in the short journey to the barn, are obviously imposed by "people looking at a computer screen dreaming up stuff." The farm keeps thirteen clipboards in the office to try to keep track of paperwork and "another dozen thick binders and manuals" for the dozen or so agencies that regulate it.

Having a clean track record is no protection against grueling regulatory intrusions. In the 2017 picking season, when the farm employed workers from Jamaica with temporary work visas, a team from the Department of Labor made a surprise inspection. The workers' papers were all in order, but the inspectors demanded twenty-two types of reports dealing with everything from vehicle registrations to time sheets, and said they would be back the next week to review them. The farm doesn't have a back office to speak of, so family members and other employees, in the middle of the busiest time of year, spent about forty hours collecting the material on wages, insurance, and immigration status. At the end of the day, all the inspectors could find were a few immaterial items of noncompliance—for example, one worker was performing tasks more relating to the farm's retail operation than agriculture. That supposedly matters because it represented a deviation from the worker's H2A visa (a program so complicated and onerous that many farmers simply resort to hiring illegal immigrants). The inspectors levied no fines, ordered that the infractions be corrected, and, after three visits, let the exhausted family return to the busy season.

The inspectors were professional, Mr. Ten Eyck's daughter Laura said, but what bothered the family was the approach of showing up periodically to try to "find something wrong." The farm had no history of being a scofflaw. Ms. Ten Eyck said she agreed with most of the regulatory goals, but longed "for a clearinghouse that would simplify the regulatory labyrinth."

Getting a permit from hydra-headed government is a similar story, except that the citizen is stymied from doing anything until all hydra heads have been satisfied. Raising the roadway of the Bayonne Bridge required forty-seven permits from nineteen different agencies. Opening a restaurant in New York, Mayor Bloomberg found, required permits from eleven different agencies. It takes so long in Illinois to approve placement for a foster child that many children "age out" of foster care before a family is found. Uncoordinated regulation accounts for the fact that the United States is now forty-ninth in World Bank rankings for ease of starting a business.

From the citizen's standpoint, it matters little where the burden comes from. Nor does it matter that each goal, viewed separately, seems reasonable. What matters is that, collectively, all these burdens are exhausting Americans—a mindless security screening line for almost any productive activity. Small business managers, doctors, teachers, and others who deal with the public increasingly can't focus on their jobs. This approach to regulating is another reason why, I believe, many Americans voted for Donald Trump.

Other countries don't tie up their citizens in red tape. Most countries in the OECD, for example, aspire to a "whole-of-government" approach and have created "one-stop shops" where a small business can go and get all the permits needed to start a business. The processes consume between a day (in New Zealand) to no more than a week (in Canada, Portugal, Germany, and other countries). In America, it can take months. Other countries also have one-stop shops for citizens to deal with social services. Portugal has eliminated most licensing laws, replacing them with after-the-fact inspections. Countries in Africa, Asia, Latin America, and the Middle East are increasingly instituting one-stop shops.

Government is supposed to serve the people, not vice versa. In America, only a few states and cities have dipped their toes into making it practical for citizens to interact with government. Mayor Mike Bloomberg, for example, created a 311 line for people to complain about government services, which has proved practically a godsend. Before 311, citizens had to navigate dense phonebooks and make multiple calls to try to find the right official—hours that often ended in failure.

Now that voters are lashing out in frustration over the accumulated burdens, it's time to reconfigure regulation to a human scale. We can draw on best practices from other countries, for example, assessing risks in order to "direct regulators' efforts at areas where it is most needed." We can also recommend pilot projects with other approaches—for example, to help citizens comply by using professionals who might be called "certified regulatory experts." Like auditors, certified experts would do periodic inspections and could help the business get into compliance. Regulation would become positive, instead of gotcha. This collaborative approach to regulation is one that OECD is recommending as having the best chance of aligning public goals with need to honor individual circumstances.

Give Responsibility to Recodification Commissions

What's needed is to push the reset button. But simplified codes cannot be drafted by Congress, for many reasons. Congress can barely do basic blocking and tackling, and its recent laws are models of opacity and complexity, not clarity. You would have thought that at some point in the last fifty years some members of Congress might have asked, "How can we do our jobs if we are unable to read or understand the proposed statutes?"

Correctness made law incoherent to everyone. The acquiescence of members of Congress to impenetrable law reflects, I'm afraid, their genuine indifference to their responsibility as lawmakers. Even without the obsessive quest to dictate correctness, however, designing simple codes would always be difficult for Congress. Statutory simplicity violates the laws of legislative physics—collecting votes requires appending favors, exceptions, and other amendments. That ends up, usually, in a tangle that looks like the tax code.

The best way to create simplified codes, probably the only way, is by appointing one or more "recodification commissions" to propose new structures. Appoint a committee to make a comprehensive proposal and then, after debate, approve some version of it. Expert committees designed the Justinian Code in the sixth century, the Napoleonic Code in the nineteenth century, the German Code at the turn of the twentieth century, and the Uniform Commercial Code in the 1950s. These were all transformative legal reforms.

Congress uses the model of independent commissions to make the politically difficult choices of which defense bases to close down. These "base closing commissions" make proposals, which Congress then has an opportunity to veto. No horse trading or complicated amendments. The inability to haggle gets individual members off the hook for failing to include some perk for a particular special interest.

Not much time should be needed for recodification commissions to do their initial work, particularly if they hew to the mandate of simplified codes focusing on public goals and frameworks for responsibility. The Simpson-Bowles Commission for balancing the budget deliberated for seven months. The proposal for what became known as the Napoleonic Code, recodifying all the laws of France, was completed by a committee of four judges in about five months. It was then debated by the legislature for a year before it voted to approve the final version. To use an example from corporate bureaucracy, it took no time at all for General Motors CEO Mary Barra to simplify its ten-page dress code to two words: "Dress appropriately."

The recodification commissions should make proposals to (1) simplify regulatory structures to revive human responsibility as the activating mechanism for public choices, and to create "one-stop shops" so that citizens can deal with one government; and (2) reset priorities, including proposals to repeal or fix obsolete programs. Historically, recodifications have energized societies weighed down by tangled legal accumulations.

Even with updated codes, however, we're still left with governing institutions that can't seem to do their jobs. I'd give the commissions two more assignments: to recommend changing how both Congress and the courts work, so they can better fulfill their responsibilities.

Fixing the Broken Branch

Just as codes must be simplified to restore human responsibility, so too Congress must be reorganized to restore responsibility to identifiable members.

Congress has a 12 percent confidence rating from the American public, lower than any other institution in society. I'm surprised the rating is that high; those citizens in the 12 percent don't understand how irresponsible Congress has become. Other than constituent service, most members of Congress might as well be performing in a high school play. They hold hearings on regulatory problems, at which I sometimes testify, but they're often just platforms for grandstanding. Not much comes out of them.

Congress has lost the capacity for action, experts say, because it has become a soapbox for partisanship. Congress was once a body in which committees had authority to roll up their sleeves and fix things. Now it is dominated, as critics Thomas Mann and Norman Ornstein explain, by powerful leaders focused on making the other side look bad. They particularly blame Republicans, who beginning in the Gingrich revolution in the mid-1990s adopted a take-no-prisoners approach that poisoned the well for actually getting together to solve problems.

What do members of Congress actually do? Most of the important decisions, say about the budget or confirming appointees, are made by leadership. For all the other members, Congress is basically organized to create the appearance of action. As comedian George Carlin put it, channeling Washington talk, they "move the process forward [to] implement the provisions of the initiative in order to meet these challenges"—i.e., they do nothing.

A proliferation of committees and subcommittees is designed to maximize chairmanships that members can tout back home. The head of Homeland Security told me he reported to almost one hundred separate committees and subcommittees.

Executive branch officials don't take Congress seriously because they know it's all for show. Hearings are for posturing, and lawmaking too is often for show—members propose "messaging bills" designed to make a point, not to actually be enacted. For example, Republicans have introduced over sixty bills to repeal or amend the Affordable Care Act, aka Obamacare.

Reporter David Fahrenthold has also sunk his teeth into the giant blob of congressional make-work. He found, for example, that Congress requires over 4,000 reports each year from 466 departments and nonprofits, including, until Fahrenthold's exposé, the Dog and Cat Fur Protection report. Another report, on the Social Security printing operation, presents Congress with such useful details as the serial number of a forklift. It's almost as if Congress, by requiring thousands of reports and hearings, is trying to divert the Executive Branch from doing its job. The report on the Social Security printing operation, Fahrenthold reports, "takes about 95 employees and 87 work-days to complete."

How can Congress be reorganized so that it can fulfill its lawmaking responsibility? Any deliberative body of 535 people will have challenges doing anything. The Framers saw this as a virtue, since there would be fewer laws. Fast-forward 230 years, and America has the opposite problem: it is crushed by the accumulation of law, and Congress can't clean it out.

Part of the solution is to shift authority back to committees. Congressman Jim Cooper describes this as going back to "regular order"—"a return to functioning committees in Congress, when members who have attended lengthy hearings hammer out legislation on a bipartisan basis, relying on their expertise more than on lobbyists." Pushing power down to committees also reduces the diffusion of accountability. At least a committee chair and ranking member will have to explain why this or that idiocy continues to exist.

A recodification commission might propose a constitutional amendment for sunsetting laws with budgetary impact. The Framers made a mistake, as I explain in *The Rule of Nobody*, by not providing a practical way to amend and repeal law. The deck is stacked against removing old programs. "Factions" do not counterbalance each other, as the Framers had hoped, but scratch each other's backs: "I'll vote for your absurd subsidy if you vote for mine."

Sunsets could be also be implemented by further expanding

the authority of congressional committees since, even in the glory days of Sam Rayburn and Howard Baker, Congress never had a great track record of dealing with old laws. Perhaps there could be a new protocol, for example, that could give committees presumptive power to amend laws within its jurisdiction—provided, say, that the change is supported by two-thirds of committee members and also by the minority leader. If those conditions were met, then Congress would automatically approve the committee's amendments. For keeping laws up to date, committees would become mini-legislatures.

Courts Must Defend the Freedom To Take Responsibility

Courts are not generally thought of as governing institutions, except for the Supreme Court. Courts are there to resolve disputes. How courts work is so well established that no living person has debated the basic conventions of modern justice. We all know the drill: anyone can sue for most accidents and disputes. An impartial judge oversees the case, and an impartial jury makes a final decision. We are taught that American justice is the fairest in the world because it has so many safeguards of impartiality.

But the facts suggest that fair justice isn't thought to be fair. Americans overwhelmingly distrust justice—only 16 percent in a 2005 Harris poll said they would trust justice to protect them against a baseless claim. The result is that a culture of defensiveness is supplanting America's can-do culture. People are paranoid about being sued. One of the casualties is responsibility: people are reluctant to take responsibility if they can get sued even when they didn't make a mistake.

Here are some ordinary choices that Americans no longer make reasonably, because of fear of lawsuits:

It's perfectly reasonable to let the nine-year-olds play in the backyard by themselves. But what if there's an accident? Pretty soon parents are hovering over children, which psychologists say stunts their emotional growth.

It's unlikely that the headache is anything but that, but who will defend the doctor if it turns out to be something serious? Better order a CT scan. Studies estimate that "defensive medicine" costs society $45–$200 billion every year.

Co-workers don't think Harry is pulling his weight, and don't like working with him. But he's the contentious type, so he may sue if he's let go. It's easier just to leave well enough alone.

There may be no serious environmental effects of this project, but one group wants to block it, so we'd better spend years doing a dense environmental review statement to defend it in litigation.

Americans didn't use to sue for the moon, or threaten lawsuits when their child got a bad grade in school. What happened? Correctness rears its head again. Justice, like government, was remade after the 1960s with the philosophy that judges should avoid making rulings of what is reasonable. Judge Charles Wyzanski enunciated the new philosophy this way: "Choosing among values is much too important a business for judges to do the choosing."

In this conception of modern justice, all decisions would be made by an impartial jury without the risk of judicial values. "Who am I to judge?" as the McDonald's hot-coffee judge asked me. So judges let people sue for almost anything, in almost any amount.

What's missing in American justice, causing this pervasive defensiveness, is the law part of lawsuits. Neither judges nor legislatures are drawing boundaries of reasonable claims. We wouldn't let a prosecutor seek the death penalty for a misdemeanor, so why did we let an angry public employee in DC sue his drycleaners for $54 million for losing a pair of pants? He lost, of course, but only after years of litigation that ruined the lives of the cleaners.

Judges should declare norms of reasonableness as a matter of law, not avoid them. Their rulings of law are how courts protect the boundaries of a free society. "Maybe you can claim $300 for your lost trousers in small claims court, but not $54 million in a court of general jurisdiction. Case dismissed." That takes about five minutes in the first hearing. That's how judges can protect the reasonable norms of a free society.

Defenders of the current system argue that they trust juries more than judges. Yes, juries are generally sensible, but juries have no authority to set precedent. Juries render ad hoc verdicts, thumbs up or thumbs down. Then the next jury is free to do exactly the opposite. So how's a person to know what's too risky? Most citizens in a free society don't want to play Russian roulette with the jury system. So they become defensive and make daily choices on the assumption that "an act is illegal," as Professor Donald Black concluded, "if it is *vulnerable* to legal action." If a town is sued for a sledding accident, no matter how

a jury decides it, then pretty soon other towns will ban sledding. After all, the next jury may not be so tolerant of the risks
of having fun.

Private lawsuits affect all of society. What people can sue
for establishes the boundaries of everyone else's freedom. In a
famous English high court opinion in 2001, Lord Hoffmann held
that common law required judges not just to consider whether
risks were foreseeable, but also rule on "the social value of the
activity which gives rise to the risk." As another judge asked,
"Does the law require that all trees be cut down because some
youths may climb them and fall?"

The reluctance of American judges to defend social norms as
a matter of law is mainly rooted in the orthodoxy about the right
to jury trial in civil cases. The Seventh Amendment provides a
constitutional right to jury trial. What that means, pretty much
everyone believes today, is that the jury must decide all issues.

But the role of juries in civil cases is to decide disputed issues
of *fact*—like who ran the red light, or is telling the truth. Juries
have no authority to decide, as a matter of *law*, whether sledding
is a reasonable risk. Because the reasonableness of sledding is
a norm that people need to "know beforehand," Justice Oliver
Wendell Holmes Jr. thought it should be decided by judges as a
matter of law and should not be "dependent upon the whim of
the particular jury."

What about "judicial activism"? Holmes's pronouncements
on the role of the judge seem flatly inconsistent with today's
accepted wisdom that judges should never be "activist." The
sin of activism, however, is for a judge to make legislative judgments about how to run jails or school systems. By contrast,

judicial rulings on the reasonableness of private claims and defenses are essential for public trust of justice. When judges sit on their hands and let litigants claim almost anything, courts can be used as a tool for extortion by any self-interested person.

Here's the fact people forget: lawsuits are not a unilateral act of freedom, but a coercive use of state power. Getting sued is just like getting indicted, except that the indictment is for money. It all comes down to a verdict where the sheriff may come and take your house away. Lawsuits are a tool of freedom, not extortion, only if judges act as gatekeepers and prevent private persons wielding the sword of state power unreasonably.

The current orthodoxy of judicial responsibility is far removed from what I've argued here. Some prominent scholars and judges agree with me, but persuading judges to draw boundaries on lawsuits will require a broader public understanding of how sue-for-anything justice undermines freedoms throughout society. A recodification commission could be charged with examining the solutions to the culture of defensiveness that is undermining Americans' freedom. If it agrees with my analysis, it could recommend a statutory or constitutional solution along these lines: "In lawsuits that may diminish reasonable freedoms of persons in society, or impede the reasonable conduct of government, judges shall make rulings of law drawing boundaries of acceptable claims and defenses."

Abject Failure of Governing Institutions

Who's in charge of American government? Here's my list of vital public choices that no one today is making:

Most laws and regulations were written decades ago, and leave little room for human judgment. America is run not by current legislators but by the officials, most long dead, who wrote these detailed dictates.

Public budgets leak massive amounts of waste from programs that everyone knows are obsolete or broken, but people in charge of Congress don't do anything about it.

Public agencies are populated by unaccountable civil servants who can't imagine any other way of governing, and take pride in their expertise about obscure procedures and rules that are impenetrable to the citizens affected by them.

Getting permits requires citizens to spend months or years navigating the shoals of a dozen or more different agencies. Enforcement is done by bureaucrats wearing blinders who are trained to insist on literal compliance, and not to use their best judgment.

Lawsuits are resolved in an ad hoc fashion, with no predictability. Unreliable justice allows justice to be gamed by people for selfish purposes, and fosters a culture of fear.

All reforms of these governing failures start with reviving individual responsibility; results must be linked to identifiable officials. I thought I had used every metaphor for government that is out of anyone's control, but then I came upon Edna St. Vincent Millay's poem, "We have gone too far" (1945). Here's an excerpt, aptly depicting the heedless way Washington governs:

...

But we, we have no sense of direction; impetus
Is all we have; we do not proceed, we only

Roll down the mountain,
Like disbalanced boulders, crushing before us many
Delicate springing things, whose plan it was to grow.

...

But we, we decide nothing: the bland Opportunity
Presents itself, and we embrace it,—we are so grateful
When something happens which is not directly War;

...

We have no sense; we only roll downhill. ...

No one is in control of modern government. No one designed it either. It's just an accidental accretion of decades of legislative and judicial decisions and compromises, piled on top of each other as every "opportunity present[ed] itself." Now this huge government boulder is rumbling and bounding down the twenty-first century. Meanwhile, "we, we decide nothing."

10

Revive the Moral Mandate

"There are no great men without virtue, and there
are no great nations . . . without respect for right."

—Alexis de Tocqueville

Bad habits are hard to change, and even harder when
America no longer has a meaningful public culture.
Tocqueville talked about it this way:

> Epochs sometimes occur in the life of a nation when
> the old customs of a people are changed, public moral-
> ity is destroyed . . . and the spell of tradition broken. . . .
> The country then assumes a dim and dubious shape in
> the eyes of the citizens. . . . The country is lost to their
> senses, . . . and they retire into a narrow and unenlight-
> ened selfishness. . . . In this predicament to retreat is
> impossible, for a people cannot recover the sentiments of
> their youth any more than a man can return to the inno-
> cent tastes of childhood; such things may be regretted but
> they cannot be renewed. They must go forward and accel-
> erate the union of private with public interests, since the
> period of disinterested patriotism is gone by forever.

Our predicament is uncomfortable. Our political muscles have atrophied. The parties are inbred, with values and ideologies that are diametrically opposed to what's needed to support a practical society. But Americans are restless and demanding change, so the status quo is not an option either.

It's little consolation that we brought it on ourselves. We tried to create a kind of automatic government, where lots of rules and processes would obviate our need to stand for particular values, or, indeed, even to pay attention. Now those supposedly neutral mechanisms are crowding out our freedoms and causing failure. We've painted ourselves into a corner. Every year the corner of our freedom gets ever smaller.

That's why Americans want to burst out. But we can't just wrap ourselves in a patriotic flag and expect shared values to permeate our culture. We need to figure this out anew, and revive a sense of personal ownership in public choices and activities.

A new governing vision grounded in human responsibility, with citizens and officials aspiring to meet public goals in their own ways, could achieve Tocqueville's proposal for a "union of private with public interests." But liberating people to take responsibility is not all that's needed. Letting people make public decisions requires a common frame of reference by which to discuss the fairness of choices, and to resolve differences by reference to shared moral principles.

Americans no longer have a shared sense of public morality. That too has atrophied. We no longer know what we're supposed to believe. A kind of moral anarchy has descended upon the land. Moral debate is dominated by fringe groups and fanatics, with no keel to keep debate centered on the common good.

We no longer believe in belief. We've been indoctrinated into believing in moral neutrality. At every level of society, people feel uncomfortable making what are pejoratively known as "value judgments." It is mandatory for judges seeking confirmation, for example, to kneel before the altar of complete neutrality and promise that they will not "make the rules" but only "apply them," as if justice were a multiple-choice test.

Relativism is practically a religion on campus, with the notable exception, of course, that victimhood is put high on a pedestal. When a friend who is a sociology professor asked his students to judge which was better—the nurturing curriculum of Montessori schools versus the relentless high-pressure Korean schools—the students reacted against making that "value judgment," even when presented with higher rates of suicide and other pathologies among Korean students.

For several decades now, thoughtful observers such as Michael Sandel have explained why moral neutrality is not only a myth but a scourge of a free society which causes our virtues to degenerate. People who want to do good have no moral authority to overcome selfishness: Who are you to judge?

Contrary to conventional wisdom, morality is not merely a matter of personal belief. Morality is the mortar of a healthy society. Man must be moral, Durkheim emphasized, "because he lives in society." Morality infuses social dealings with mutual trust. People are able to achieve more when they trust others to abide by shared norms of fairness, such as the Golden Rule directive to "do unto others . . ." Truthfulness is essential for trust. Norms of sharing and restraint are essential for stewardship of scarce common resources—including protecting clean air and water, and allocating finite public budgets in schools and government.

A culture of people aspiring to do what's right will have more "social capital." Social capital is like money in the bank. Mutual trust in a shared vision inspires people. It gives meaning to activities independent of economic considerations. You can do so much more with yourself, and with your community, and everyone else can as well. Cultures with more social capital, such as the Centers for Disease Control where employees volunteer for hazardous assignments, are able to achieve high levels of institutional performance and personal fulfillment.

Every joint activity depends upon shared values. "Between 'can do' and 'may do,'" a British law lord once observed, "exist[s] the whole realm which recognizes the sway of duty, fairness, sympathy, taste and all the other things that make life beautiful and society possible."

Adherence to moral virtues was considered by the Framers as an essential element of a successful democracy. They were explicit about the human tendency towards selfishness, and created a framework where people would act as checks on each other. But they also understood that people want to do good, and believed that the success of democracy hinged on shared social values putting the common good ahead of selfish goals. "Only a virtuous people," Benjamin Franklin observed, "are capable of freedom." Thomas Jefferson suggested that we must affirmatively enforce good values: "No government can continue good but under the controul of the people . . . encouraged in habits of virtue, & deterred from those of vice."

Conventional wisdom is that Americans no longer share

the same values. Indeed, people do have many differences in values—including work habits, ways of communicating, humor, attire, political views, and, above all, different cultural traditions.

The core values needed for a healthy society, however, are not optional. These are values of truthfulness, reciprocity, and loyalty to the common good. We must demand them in all social dealings, and hold accountable those who refuse to abide by them.

American culture has frayed in large part because we made those core values optional. Disabling moral judgments about right and wrong has steadily dissipated America's social capital. Here is what moral neutrality has unleashed in America:

A culture of selfishness.
Public selfishness, Edmund Burke believed, spells the end of free society: "Men are qualified for civil liberty in exact proportion to their disposition to put moral chains upon their own appetites."

The supposedly neutral rules of correctness have transformed law into a vehicle for self-interest. The rights revolution, for example, has degenerated into demands for personal gain. How did it happen that lousy teachers have a "right" to keep teaching our children? What about the students' rights?

Selfishness is a contagious disease. Once people start grabbing for themselves, others do as well. Distrust replaces sharing and helpfulness. Distrust breeds fear, causing people to act defensively instead of feeling free to act on their best judgment. People retreating into defensive foxholes lose their sense of ownership for society. The common enterprise starts to disintegrate. "A brackish tide of pessimism," columnist David Brooks observes, "turns into passivity," and "people are quick to decide that longstanding problems . . . are intractable and not really worth taking on."

Overgrazing the commons.

A moral society requires fidelity to the future. As Frederick Douglass put it, "You have no right to enjoy. . . the labors of your fathers, unless your children are to be blest by your labors."

Washington no longer feels a duty of responsible stewardship for the future. Budget deficits mean that our children will pay the tab for Washington's refusal to fix wasteful programs. Obsolete programs stay in place because, well, some interest groups want to keep them. We are living on infrastructure built by our grandparents and great-grandparents, and can't modernize it because Democrats won't cut red tape and Republicans won't raise taxes to fund it.

Political debate is about self-interest, not competing visions of the common good. Politics "lacks moral resonance," as Michael Sandel puts it, and is replaced by appeals to personal gain. Republicans claim that tax cuts will stimulate the economy, but the subtext is that tax cuts will help rich supporters. Democrats argue that individual rights are critical for a just society, but what they really mean is that they will help public unions and other political supporters. Absolutist policy positions deny the need for balance—"No New Taxes!" is the natural companion to "Give Me My Rights!"

The irresponsibility of political leaders is matched by the anti-responsibility of civil servants. Officials worry about avoiding blame instead of getting things done. The surest way to get in trouble is to actually do something. Far safer to retreat into legal process. The proposed new power line is needed to access wind power, but who will defend the official when the farmers complain about unsightly power poles? Better to do a few thousand more pages of environmental review.

Washington has sold out the future of our society. We are living off the investments of our ancestors, while bequeathing our children the debt of our profligate entitlements. Without a vocabulary of public morality, few people even pay attention. Advocates of fiscal restraint, such as Pete Peterson and Paul Volcker, are politely ignored.

What you believe doesn't matter.
Most people want to do what's right, and feel pride in their work and in their role in the community. But morality needs to be honored, not treated as a foolhardy gesture by the weak. All around us, in politics, in the community, and in social media, we see people with antisocial values who are not called to account. People demand as much as possible for themselves, without regard for others. Bad attitudes, bad morals, and untruthfulness have no consequences. Self-absorbed people have a kind of competition for the greatest narcissist. The Kardashians are famous for . . . being famous.

Relativism grew out of justifiable guilt over bad social values, such as racism and gender discrimination. We were taught, as Michael Polanyi put it, that "to refrain from belief is always an act of intellectual probity." But what we accomplished was not a fairer society, but one dominated by groups more than willing to fill the vacuum with their own values. "Fundamentalists rush in," as Michael Sandel put it, "where liberals fear to tread."

Relativism is an abdication of basic norms needed for a civilized society. The goal was to replace bad values with neutral rules, but this amorality opened the door to selfishness and inevitably degenerated into immorality. The erosion of mutual trust unleashed a downward spiral of destructive conduct. At this point, facts have lost their authority. Disregard for reality is not confined to fringe groups in their echo chambers—whether right-wing extremists or public unions defending indefensible abuses. Flagrant falsehood is now an accepted technique of partisan debate by our political leaders, including, profligately, by President Trump. When what's true doesn't matter, all basis for social trust disappears. American culture is transformed into an "anti-culture." The harm is not just to our public institutions, but, ultimately, to our own ability to function effectively in society. Hannah Arendt explained: "The result of a consistent . . . substitution of lies for factual truth is not that the lies will now be accepted . . . but that the sense by which we take our bearings in the real world . . . is being destroyed."

Tools for a Moral Society

Morality is demonstrated by acts, not talk or intent. "To act morally is to do good to beings of flesh and blood," Durkheim said, "to change something in reality."

Because good values are manifested in actions, they cannot be prescribed in advance or even predicted. It all boils down to the judgment of the person with responsibility. Fair discipline in a classroom requires a teacher who knows the students and the situation to make a judgment. A fair personnel decision requires a supervisor who knows the people involved. Fair legislation requires Congress to consider the extent of the need and competing uses of scarce public dollars.

Not every choice works out well, of course, and not every choice can be put under a microscope and judged. People with responsibility make countless choices daily. One of the errors of legal correctness is its atomistic approach to accountability—focusing the microscope on one decision, out of context. Demanding perfection, as philosopher Onora O'Neill suggests, is like pulling up a plant to examine its roots. Both accountability and morality must generally be evaluated by observing what a pattern of conduct reveals about a person, including that person's character.

Character Judgments Are the Main Tool of a Moral Society

The trust needed for social capital is generally trust in people's character. When judging someone, we take into account the person's overall track record. People earn reputations for fairness, forthrightness, and dedication to the mission of the common enterprise. The character of a person, not a particular decision, is what embodies his morality. "All acts are so tied together," John Dewey explained, "that any one of them may have to be judged as an expression of character."

We naturally gravitate towards people of good character, and away from others. Dewey considered evaluations of character to be critical to our success in life. That's how we decide who to deal with—to do business with people we trust and avoid people we don't.

It's a mistake to equate moral character with a form of niceness or avoidance of vices. Character requires backbone more than niceness. A nice person can act immorally by going along with selfish demands, or refusing to make hard decisions, as officials in Washington do.

Character is manifested in action. Reorganizing government by scope of responsibility lets character and leadership emerge free of the legal tangle. "The freedom of the subjective person to do as he pleases," Polanyi emphasizes, "is overruled by the freedom of the responsible person to act as he must." Today, by contrast, leadership might as well be illegal. Any naysayer can pull the rug out from under a potential leader by invoking correctness. Can you prove your decision is fair?

Building a moral society requires, first, allegiance to the principle that morality is the foundation of social trust. Moral character is then revealed when people take responsibility. Their actions will demonstrate commitment to the common good instead of self-interest. People with character and judgment attract followers and become leaders. These leaders inspire others and instill trust that moral values will be honored. The stock of social capital rises.

A moral society is almost impossible unless people have the ability to take responsibility. In a speech before Congress, Václav Havel tried to explain: "We are still incapable of understanding that the only genuine core of all our actions—if they are to be moral—is responsibility."

In small ways and great ways, people with moral character can lead a fractured society back to moral health. But first they must be empowered to take responsibility. At the conclusion of *Democracy in America,* Tocqueville emphasized that strong individuals are needed to make a strong society:

> It would seem as if the rulers of our time sought only to use men in order to make things great; I wish that they would try a little more to make great men; . . . that they would never forget that a nation cannot long remain strong when every man belonging to it is individually weak; and that no form or combination of social polity has yet been devised to make an energetic people out of a community of . . . enfeebled citizens.

A Moral Society Requires Sanctions

The second essential tool of a moral society, after judgments about character, is imposing social sanctions. Morality has no teeth if antisocial behavior has no consequences.

To people steeped in relativism, the idea of sanctions seems almost barbaric. But Durkheim defined morality as "social norms and rules which are accompanied by sanctions giving them a certain coercive power." Selfish or immoral acts are usually enforced by social consequences rather than law—by public shame, for example, or loss of social or business relationships.

There's a natural inclination towards tolerance. But we have taken tolerance to an extreme. University presidents who refuse to defend faculty members against student bullies are complicit in encouraging antisocial conduct. Our passivity, I think, is less about tolerance than cowardice. Social critic

Christopher Lasch put his finger on our timidity to call out people for bad behavior:

> We are determined to respect everyone, but we have forgotten that respect has to be earned. Respect is not another word for tolerance or the appreciation of 'alternative lifestyles and communities.' This is a tourist's approach to morality. Respect is what we experience in the presence of admirable achievements, admirably formed characters, natural gifts put to good use. It entails the exercise of discriminating judgement, not indiscriminate acceptance.... It is our reluctance to make demands on each other, much more than our reluctance to help those in need, that is sapping the strength of democracy today.

Moral responsibility will not be taken seriously unless people who act irresponsibly suffer the consequences of their actions. The proof is always in the pudding. Is this person dedicated to the mission, and does he act in a way we respect and trust? Or is he self-serving?

Today in America many people think that the way to get ahead is to demand more for themselves. Robert Reich wants to revive shaming as an essential tool of a free society. He's clearly correct: if we believe in morality, then we have to stand up for it. Shaming should be used not for policy differences, however—that's bullying, as we see on campuses, and denies core values of mutual respect. The book to read is *The Coddling of the American Mind*, by Greg Lukianoff and Jonathan Haidt.

Local Responsibility Enhances Morality

Public morality is far easier to achieve on a local level, where people can deal with officials who live in the community and who can be more readily accountable for unfair or inequitable decisions. When confronted with a real problem, or the reality of a budget constraint, people can make practical compromises. They begin to see the virtue of shared moral norms. As political scientist Francis Fukuyama explains, "They develop an interest in their own reputations, as well as in the monitoring and punishment of those who violate community rules." That's why government must be brought to a human scale.

A successful democracy, Tocqueville said, should aspire not to efficiency but to the energy of citizen ownership: "Democracy does not give the people the most skillful government, but it produces . . . an all-pervading and restless activity . . . which may . . . produce wonders." Centralized administration, by contrast, "is fit only to enervate, . . . by incessantly diminishing their local spirit."

The allocation of responsibility between central dictates and local control can be determined, under a doctrine called "subsidiarity," by allocating responsibility to the lowest practical level. Instead of rigidly controlling social services, for example, government should encourage any responsible human intervention. Letting churches, synagogues, and local charities take more responsibility for social services not only enhances the social capital of a community, but holds the promise of beginning to deal with intractable social problems. For example, organizing a nurturing environment for young unmarried mothers and infants is more likely to engage both mother and volunteers if done informally rather than in a bureaucratic straitjacket. Community Solutions, a nonprofit, has helped dozens of communities dramatically reduce chronic homelessness by bringing local groups and officials together under one roof to deal with the unique issues presented by each homeless person.

Liberals tend to distrust localism because, well, what if the town teaches creationism? But subsidiarity, unlike federalism, does not cede all power. Subsidiarity accepts central oversight, and allows a local official who goes rogue to be reined in or replaced. Subsidiarity originated in the Roman Catholic Church on the basis that moral choices can best be determined by people on the ground. Subsidiarity is now a core governing principle in the European Union.

The transformative potential of subsidiarity is not in autonomy, at least not in the do-whatever-you-want sense, but in restoring the opportunities for self-determination. Columnist Tom Friedman described how Lancaster, Pennsylvania, experienced a renaissance over the past decade when citizens got together and decided to take ownership for the city's future. Fruitful programs emerged almost spontaneously as citizens sat around kitchen tables. A nonprofit was formed that "mobilizes citizens to contribute time and resources to build and repair affordable housing." The local hospital and college formed a partnership to revive the street that connects them. A church noticed that many underprivileged children were dropped off early for school and organized a program to serve them breakfast. A basic change in approach, Friedman found, is that citizens and officials no longer organize themselves in legal silos; real people take responsibility to do what's needed to get to the desired result. The growth of social capital in Lancaster almost seems contagious, growing when citizens see other citizens making a difference. As with any successful enterprise, "The key to it all is trust," as one civic leader said. "People trust that we are not in it for personal agendas and not partisan agendas."

Move Government Out of Washington

Giving communities more responsibility leaves the problem that Washington is still pulling many strings, making judgments about when and how to intervene, and will still have a congenital aversion to letting people do things in their own way. This leads me to one last suggestion for bringing federal government closer to the people, which would shake things up almost immediately: Start moving agencies out of Washington. This is less daunting than you might think. Companies move all the time.

Cultures with embedded habits, like individuals with habits, are hard to change. All the ligaments and tendons of Washington's permanent apparatus—civil servants, lobbyists, lawyers, contractors, media, and politicians—are conditioned to play their roles in its giant bureaucratic apparatus. Big change is literally inconceivable to them: "Why, no, that's not how we do things here." The million or so public employees, lobbyists, and other stakeholders are dug in. Civil servants have a phrase for resisting any efforts at change: "WEBEHWYGs" (pronounced WEE-BEE-WIGS), or "We'll be here when you're gone."

How can we govern sensibly or morally when officials in

Washington refuse to change direction? The answer is that we can't. We must confront this reality. Why fight this culture head on? Start moving agencies out of Washington to places where people are not afraid of taking responsibility. The FDA could move to Boston or San Diego, both cities with a cohort of scientists. HUD could go to Detroit. Some people might move with the agencies, but not most. Congress and the White House could stay in Washington, with the foreign policy apparatus.

Modern communications have removed the need for government to be in one place. Federal agencies located outside Washington, as we see with the Centers for Disease Control in Atlanta, seem to get the job done. The cost of replacing 75 percent of federal offices in Washington is literally a drop in the bucket—a one-time charge of about 1 percent of the annual federal budget. Washington has demonstrated that it can't do its job. Why not give federal government back to localities as well?

Bringing government closer to the ground can only inspire a higher level of engagement and morality. It's useful to remember that democracy is supposed to be government by the people, not by distant bureaucrats.

11

Profile of a Practical Society

"The ideal of true freedom is ... for all
members of human society alike
to make the best of themselves."

—Thomas Hill Green

y vision for a new governing philosophy ultimately
rests on the dignity and responsibility of each person. Waking up each morning, each of us must have
the option of fulfilling public responsibilities in our own way.
We must have the joy and tension of convincing others that we
are trustworthy and effective.

The magnitude of the needed overhauls is a manifestation of
how intrusive legal correctness has become. The giant bureaucratic edifice must be abandoned, and replaced by simpler
frameworks activated by people taking responsibility.

The spring-cleaning of legacy bureaucracies is an occasion to
purge unnecessary waste and approach old problems in a more
practical way. A little humility is permitted when we see that
the quest for perfection didn't work out. By acknowledging the
impossibility of curing all social ills, we can bring government

back towards terra firma. Government can't mandate perfect fairness or perfect anything. A thousand rules, or even a million, can't achieve a caring nursing home, or a safe workplace, or a successful school. These endeavors are uniquely and self-evidently dependent on the humans involved.

Complex social ills will never be cured with money and the stroke of a pen. Progress, not nirvana, is the realistic aspiration for most social programs. Regulation is aimed at avoiding error and abuse, not purging them. That doesn't mean government shouldn't strive for difficult public goals. But it must do so in a practical way, mindful of resource limitations, opportunity costs, conflicting public goals, and, most importantly, the absolute certainty that the program will not work out as planned.

It would be hard not to improve upon the dense legal codes that, today, squander public funds and suffocate daily freedoms. Pushing the reset button will not only transform government, but will unleash productive activity throughout society. Here are a few snapshots of how government and society should work differently.

Regulators police unsafe conduct, not correctness. Regulation will be more effective, and less disruptive, when regulators and citizens alike focus on avoiding actual harm. Creating one-stop shops will foster entrepreneurship and improve regulatory compliance. Radically simplifying codes will improve regulatory understanding. Instead of 4,000 rules dictating how to run a safe workplace, for example, the worker safety law should set goals and general principles. Instead of getting fined for trivial errors such as inadequate paperwork, the farmer or factory foreman can at least try to explain to an inspector why a situation is not hazardous. If the inspector disagrees and declares a violation, the citizen can appeal up the hierarchy, and, ultimately, to a court. Today, by contrast, the impossibility of complying with thousands of rules means the government has arbitrary authority to impose whatever penalty it wants.

Government is accountable. When civil servants are accountable, the internal culture of public offices will be energized by mutual trust and commitment. By delegating public choices to communities, and reconnecting the rungs of the hierarchy, democracy will become an active mechanism for citizen input. If officials have a track record of being unreasonable, they can be terminated. Elections will matter.

Public schools have similar freedoms as charter schools. Instead of smothering teachers and principals with mandates, metrics, and union rigidities, the new framework will fling open the legal doors and windows, and let educators take responsibility again. Teachers will be able to draw on their personalities and use spontaneity to engage the interest of students. Principals will have authority over discipline and staffing—with safeguards against unfairness provided by a parent-teacher oversight committee, not due process legal hearings. Washington will give block grants instead of micromanaging schools, and will use the power of the purse to dislodge teachers' union intransigence— no grants until ineffective teachers can be removed.

Doctors focus on care, not metrics and paperwork. To liberate doctors and nurses to focus on patient care, the legal and reimbursement landscape should be cleared out. Codes should become simplified so that important protocols, such as pre-surgery checklists, receive more emphasis. Reimbursement paperwork should be minimized by moving to integrated care providers such as Kaiser or other "capitated" reimbursement systems. Today doctors waste up to half their time on paperwork, much of it to justify the reimbursement for more care. Special health courts should be created to restore reliability to medical justice and avoid the waste of $45–$200 billion in unnecessary "defensive medicine."

The workplace isn't a legal minefield. It's hard to develop camaraderie and trust when any criticism or spontaneity can spring a trapdoor into a vat of legal tar. It seems odd that, in the land of the First Amendment, most employers have a policy to not give job references for former employees, no matter how good or how bad. In a society where people are supposed to be free, supervisors and workers should not generally worry about law in daily work interactions except for two workplace taboos: systematic discrimination and sexual harassment. Accountability is key to a healthy workplace culture, not an act that should be laden with legal danger.

Children are allowed to run around. Children in other countries actually wander outside, play games where someone loses, and spend hours with other children without adult supervision. What this does, according to child development experts, is teach them to be resourceful in taking risks, dealing with others, and generally taking care of themselves. We must remove the bubble wrap, and allow children to be children again. This requires one cultural change—parents should no longer hover—

and one legal change—judges must not allow lawsuits for accidents that occur in normal play.

Social work and volunteer help is encouraged, not constrained. Helping people is more important than regulating how the help is given. Government should safeguard against crazy schemes and people, not go ballistic over inadequate paperwork, or home-cooked meals, or if a volunteer in a faith-based group uses the G-word.

Citizens in a free society should be free to judge other people, including about their moral character. A culture where people are valued for their character and commitment is hard to maintain if we can't act on our judgments about people who don't uphold those values. People judging people is the currency of a moral society as well as of a healthy workplace.

Federal government is no longer a separate, inbred culture. The inbred culture of Washington, with permanent castes of current and former officials, lobbyists, and companies feeding at the trough, will be disrupted and exposed to the fresh breezes of the goals and values of the rest of the country. Agencies will no longer huddle together in an unaccountable fortress in Washington but will be dispersed around the country and repopulated by people willing to take responsibility. Civil service will no longer be a lifetime sentence but will be open to idealistic graduates willing to do public service for a few years. Congress will not be an unaccountable black box but will be reorganized into committees subject to the scrutiny of citizens for how their laws actually work.

Eliminating the waste of legacy bureaucracies releases vast public resources for current needs. Clunky government programs, built decades ago with rigid structures that preclude practical choices, squander public resources as well as frustrate Americans. Simplifying programs to be goals-oriented will not only improve their performance but will make available public resources to promote fiscal responsibility and address new needs.

The basic shift here is away from dense codes towards an open framework that allows officials and citizens freedom to meet their obligations in their own way. This shift in governing approach is dramatic, but it should not be frightening. There are no more master dictates emanating from Washington. Instead of being dictated by rules, each public choice must ultimately rest on responsible humans. For most decisions that affect you, government will be represented by a real person, right in front of you, whose job it is to make sense of decisions for the common good.

Tocqueville in his book *The Old Regime and the Revolution* found that one of the main causes of the French Revolution was stifling control by central government of the smallest details of life in the countryside. The traditional feudal hierarchy of local nobles had atrophied, with nobility fleeing to Paris to be near the center of power in the court. Here are some of Tocqueville's descriptions of how citizens in the countryside and provincial cities received dictates from a distant power:

> This habit of surveillance became almost an obsession with the central government. Towards the close

of the eighteenth century it was impossible to arrange for poor-relief work in the humblest village of a province hundreds of miles from the capital without the Controller-General's insisting on having his say about the exact sum to be expended, the site of the workhouse, and the way it was to be managed.... A most elaborate machinery had to be set up for coping with the flood of documents that poured in from all sides, and even so the delays of the administration were notorious. On studying the records I found that it took a year at least for a parish to get permission to repair a church steeple or the priest's house. Oftener than not the time required was much longer: two or three years.... In the recriminatory tone of a letter written by a farmer ... we sense something of the spirit of the impending revolution.

'Why does government not appoint inspectors to tour the provinces once a year and examine the condition of the crops and explain to the cultivators how to improve them, how to rear their cattle, fatten them and sell them, and at what places they can count on the best markets? These inspectors should draw good salaries and the farmer producing the best crops in each district should be given a badge of merit.'

Does any of this sound familiar? Peter and Laura Ten Eyck at Indian Ladder Farms could readily identify with the plight of the eighteenth-century farmer in France. Dictating stupid rules at a distance will be endured only so long. Washington doesn't seem to realize it, but it's sitting on top of a volcano.

No one in Washington will willingly accept a recodification commission or other proposed reforms—these changes will disrupt and put at risk the cherished legal benefits for 5,000-odd interest groups. Nor will reform come with negotiation or political horse-trading. Small thinking is the common sin of Washington reformers. Real reform will come only by overwhelming public pressure. This will require a new party, new leaders, and a new vision of governing.

Although it's hard for us to acknowledge, Washington has become our enemy. The fact that most people there mean well can't disguise the reality of ineffective, overbearing, and wasteful programs, or the inability of the huge bureaucratic apparatus to respond to the goals of American citizens. Washington is little different in this regard than the hidebound courts of George III, Louis XVI, Czar Nicholas II, or other regimes that failed because they refused to heed the needs of their citizens. We should not try to avoid conflict with Washington but should embrace it. Every broken program is another reason to create a new governing framework. Every indignity of mindless bureaucracy is another weapon in our arsenal for humiliating those who resist a new framework of responsibility.

12

Who Has Responsibility for Change?

"Human greatness . . . exists only
for those committed to [it]."

—Michael Polanyi

Change is coming. That's the signal of the Trump election. But the Democratic and Republican parties seem unable to respond to growing voter anger. Instead of changing how they work, both parties have doubled down on gridlock.

There seem to be two voter groups in America. The prosperous elites who live on the east and west coasts are inclined to hang on to the status quo; after all, they have the most to lose by any disruption. The heartland wants change.

I believe the heartland will win. Look at what's happening around the world. Countries that recently reveled in new freedoms, such as Hungary, Poland, and Turkey, are embracing semi-totalitarian leaders. Buffeted by forces of global commerce, people all over the world are attracted to strong leaders who can make trains run on time. These authoritarian leaders, like their predecessors in the 1930s, come with baggage that usually tears a culture apart—justifying their power by inciting fear of "the other," whether immigrants, ethnic groups, or "fake news" by the media.

What is driving people into the arms of totalitarian leaders? One thing more than any other—the ineptitude of modern democracies. Ineptitude at the top always spreads through society like an infectious disease. The ancient historian Polybius viewed the disintegration of democracy into dictatorship as inevitable, because of the tendency of democratic leaders to overspend finite resources to the point of fiscal collapse. He did not foresee the additional defect, as Tocqueville did, that democracy would suffocate society under "a network of small complicated rules, minute and uniform, through which the most original minds and the most energetic characters cannot penetrate."

The bureaucratic systems of modern democracies will ultimately fail. The bureaucratic state can't make decisions, can't provide public services effectively, can't be responsive, and can't protect people from economic fear. Bureaucratic rigidity squanders taxpayer money in virtually every public program. Worst, perhaps, the bureaucratic state disempowers people from solving problems on their own. Sorry, the rules don't allow it.

The open question, then, is whether democracies will also fail. America is obviously not immune to the attraction of strongmen.

My proposal is to give democracy another chance. Let's learn from our mistakes and abandon the utopian dream of a legally correct society. Give Americans back their freedom to do things, as Frank Sinatra would say, "my way." Let everyone

make choices within the scope of their responsibility, accountable to those up the hierarchy. That's how the Framers intended
democracy to work. Madison, Hamilton, Jefferson, and especially George Washington would be aghast at the dense, anti-
human bureaucracy. They aspired to public choices that are
practical and moral, not rigid centralized dictates.

America's constitutional framework relies upon human
responsibility as the mechanism for implementing public
choices. It's hard to imagine any superior alternative. Our
experiment with legal correctness after the 1960s didn't work
out—indeed, is fomenting voter revolt—so going back to basics
seems prudent.

There's also another reason to walk away from the current
system: Governing without human responsibility is immoral.
It is wasteful of tax dollars, and, worse, uses future resources
to pay for wastefulness today. It has unleashed a plague of selfishness upon the land, seen every day in people pounding the
table for their so-called rights, with almost no discussion about
the common good. It deprives each of us of moral ambitions and
meaning. It deters us from joining with others to create something greater than ourselves. This system is amoral by design,
and immoral in effect. By preempting human responsibility, it
precludes moral choices at every level of society.

Replacing this system is the right thing to do. Automatic government gave us a kind of vacation from democratic responsibility for a few decades, but now it's time to confront its failures
before someone unreliable does it for us. As Havel told the
Czech people, their acceptance of the communist regime "as an
unalterable fact . . . helped to perpetuate it. . . . None of us is just
its victim: We are all also its co-creators."

Organizing a popular movement might seem inconceivably hard. The massive state has deadened our public spirit. Americans have become passive owners of democracy, with no muscle memory of how to organize for reform. As if hit by a bureaucratic neutron bomb, America has been atomized into powerless individuals with almost no ability to take public responsibility.

Movements are not so daunting. They're social activities. Get together with friends. See how they feel. If you're roughly on the same page, then you can expand the discussion to others. Reform groups can act as a resource, and community groups can provide meeting places as the discussion expands. Social media can be used to accelerate the gathering. Leaders will emerge. A new party or movement will coalesce.

Reform movements usually need a villain. Do you think Washington will change how it works? Look again. Persuading Washington is hopeless. Wandering into that swamp with a machete, even with the bluster of Donald Trump, is a fool's errand. No one there can conceive of governing with human responsibility. Like creatures never exposed to sunlight, officials in Washington have the unhealthy pallor of people cut off from public goals. What procedure do we follow now? Washington is more Huxley than Orwell, more lassitude than evil, a culture where, as in *Brave New World*, the ultimate sin is to have "a conception of purpose." Washington must be abandoned, literally and figuratively.

America needs a new governing vision. My vision is this: I believe in a practical society. I believe in a public sphere where officials take responsibility and are accountable to others for how they do. I believe in our capacity to judge good from evil, and to act accordingly. I believe in virtue, which promotes trust, which liberates human potential. I believe in the upward arc of the human spirit, not the downward spiral of suffocating legalisms. I make this proposal: Put humans in charge.

Belief can change a society if it is widely shared. We must believe in ourselves, and in our capacity to engage with others to achieve practical action. Belief is the core asset of a free society. Demand that officials do what's right. Demand it of yourself, and of those around you. That's what I hope will drive this movement. "There is an amazing strength," Tocqueville observed, "in the expression of the will of a whole people."

Everyone knows the current system is broken. No one in power will fix it. It's unfixable. Correctness precludes common sense and preserves the past. Responsibility opens the door to the future, letting people apply their energies to make a difference. We must replace this failed system. That's our responsibility. Who else is going to do it?

APPENDIX

Ten Principles for a Practical Society

AMERICA NEEDS A NEW OPERATING PHILOSOPHY built on the bedrock of individual responsibility and accountability. Rebuilding a governing framework on that core principle will transform society: Americans can make things work again; apathy will disappear, replaced by the knowledge that you and others can make a difference; trust will start to build when there's a backdrop of accountability; democracy will be energized when leaders have the room to try new approaches. Public debate and private debate will also be transformed: People will argue over what's the right thing to do, not parse legal language or demand self-interested rights.

The following principles focus on how public choices are made, not what the priorities of modern government should be. Bringing choices down to the ground will allow people to solve problems in a practical way instead of fighting over abstract theories. Studies show that people with sharply different political views usually agree on the right thing to do in a particular situation.

Each of these principles is grounded in one simple idea: People must be empowered to achieve public goals sensibly and fairly, and be accountable for how they do. Law will become a framework, and no longer be an instruction manual. For public choices, officials and citizens should be free to act on this question: what's the right thing to do here?

Principle One: Restore Individual Responsibility. Regulatory structures must be radically simplified to provide goals, guiding principles, and a hierarchy of responsibility. The focus must be on public goals, not detailed dictates on how to achieve them. The structure must define the scope of responsibility for citizens and officials in a way that gives them ample room to achieve these goals.

Examples: Designated officials should be authorized to make decisions on permits if agencies with overlapping jurisdiction cannot agree.

Detailed rules should be used only when rigidity and uniformity are more practical than flexibility—for example, speed limits, or a checklist protocol before surgery.

Principle Two: Revive Individual Accountability. Officials must be accountable based on judgment of supervisors and co-workers, without legal proceedings except in cases of misconduct. Personal accountability is essential for a functioning democracy, and also for a healthy institutional culture. Accountability provides an essential backdrop for mutual trust; people can fulfill their responsibilities with reasonable assurance that others will do the same.

Examples: The standard for personnel decisions should not be due process, but what's best for the common good. Government should aspire to excellence, not the bare minimum. Accountability always requires judgment, and cannot be compartmentalized into metrics or objective proof.

Overhaul civil service. Civil service should be remade to

provide neutral hiring, but not tenure. Collective bargaining by public unions should be abolished on grounds that it is unconstitutional infringement of executive power under Article II of the Constitution, and also on policy grounds. Aside from supervisory misconduct, the only legal protection against termination should be review by an independent board to guard against politically motivated termination (as was provided in the Lloyd-Lafollette Act).

Use federal spending power and new legal theories to dislodge the iron grip of state and local public unions and teachers unions. States and localities should abolish collective bargaining and, instead, appoint periodic review commissions to recommend changes in compensation and work rules.

Principle Three: Bureaucracy Is Evil. Slavish attention to rules, metrics, and objective proof dehumanize government. Bureaucracy causes failure by disabling human ingenuity and willpower. Bureaucracy polarizes society by preventing people from dealing flexibly with each other and the problem at hand. Bureaucracy suffocates the human spirit in every setting, causing burnout and alienation. Bureaucracy causes unfairness by encouraging people to "game" the rules for selfish purposes. Bureaucracy is too dense to be understood by those expected to abide by it. Bureaucratic structures must be abandoned and replaced by ones grounded in human responsibility.

Principle Four: Reboot Government Programs. Few government programs work as intended. Many are obsolete. They need to be repealed or rebuilt in light of current needs, and to replace bureaucratic micromanagement with a simpler framework of human responsibility. Congress should authorize recodification commissions to propose new codes, including new agency regulations.

Examples: Create one-stop shops for small business and citizens. The multiplicity of agencies is impossible for small businesses to navigate. These one-stop shops should have the job of coordinating regulatory requirements for different businesses, such as farms, restaurants, and other small businesses.

Experiment with privatizing regulatory enforcement, with "certified regulatory experts" serving a similar role as certified public accountants.

For many regulatory goals, such as patient privacy, substitute a "rule of reason" standard instead of perfect compliance. Often people can accomplish 95 percent of the goal for a fraction the cost and diversion of energy. With health care, freeing up those human resources can achieve better health care.

Principle Five: Appoint Recodification Commissions with the Job of Proposing New Codes in Each Area. Congress can then vote a recodification proposal up or down. To avoid partisan politics to the extent possible, the leadership of Congress should appoint outside experts to nominate members of the recodification commissions.

Principle Six: Courts Must Defend Boundaries of Reasonableness. What people can sue for establishes the boundaries of everyone else's freedom. Judges must act as gatekeepers, dismissing or limiting claims that might interfere with the freedoms of all citizens. For example, letting parents sue a teacher who restrained a misbehaving student will lead to future disorder as students correctly read the teachers' lack of authority.

Examples: Congress should create expert health courts to restore reliability and trust in malpractice litigation. Every year, doctors waste an estimated $45–$200 billion in "defensive medicine." The resulting lack of candor means that the quality of care is also compromised.

Congress should appoint a special committee to recommend guidelines on children's play and autonomy. In part because of fear of litigation, child development experts say America's children are not given the challenges needed to learn how to be resourceful as adults. In the words of one expert, we are creating a "nation of wimps."

Principle Seven: Reorganize Congress. Congress has abdicated its responsibility to oversee whether laws and regulations are serving the public good. Changes include giving committees authority to amend programs when certain conditions are met; sunsetting all laws with budgetary impact, and requiring a public report by an independent body before any program is reauthorized; and giving Congress authority, by constitutional amendment if necessary, to veto agency regulations created under statute.

Principle Eight: Give Communities Ownership of Local Services. Federal mandates for schools and social services should be turned into broad principles, with leeway for communities to provide the services in their own way. Special education, for example, is notoriously bureaucratic and leaves little room for balancing the needs of all students. Letting people make a difference in their own communities will awaken citizen commitment to the common good.

Principle Nine: Move Agencies out of Washington. The bureaucratic culture of Washington is so inbred that it is unlikely that most people there can adjust to taking responsibility to achieve goals. In the age of instant communication, there is no reason why most agencies should be in Washington. Combined with breaking apart the monopoly of civil service, moving agencies will allow government to be run by Americans not afraid to take responsibility.

Principle Ten: The Litmus Test for Public Choices Must Be the Common Good. Every public dollar involves a moral choice: spend it on an obsolete subsidy from the New Deal, and it is not available to provide prenatal care to an underprivileged mother. Rights have become a synonym for selfishness. Constitutional rights should return to their role as protecting freedom against state coercion, not a tool of coercion for one person over another. No one should have rights superior to anyone else.

ACKNOWLEDGMENTS

Many friends and colleagues helped me during the five-month sprint writing this book. Dennis Zhou dived in fresh out of grad school at Oxford and was invaluable, compiling reams of resources and revealing editorial judgment far beyond his years. Professor Jonathan Friedman was able to pull together prodigious learning and populist anti-learning to provide the foundation for several important arguments, and was an informed sounding board.

Andy Park, the head of research at Common Good, is wonderfully thoughtful and principled, and I'll always treasure our arguments on hard issues here. The rest of the team from Common Good lent their expertise in different areas, particularly David Choi on public employment and education, Matt Brown on infrastructure, and Josh Ferguson on finding the pulse of the country. Ron Faucheux is my reality check on how Washington works and thinks. Henry Miller is invaluable as a communications adviser, with lots of help from Donna Thompson and Emma McKinstry. Ruth Giverin and Kyle Khachadurian kept the trains running on time.

For international law, I am grateful to Professor James

Maxeiner, whose comparative work should be mined for ideas on how agencies can better deliver services. Nick Malyshev and Daniel Trnka at OECD were generous in providing materials and discussing the efficacy of different approaches. Professors Robert Heineman and Daniel DiSalvo commented on different sections.

My colleagues at Covington & Burling are always available to help with their expertise and to open doors, and I'm particularly grateful to E. Donald Elliott for his help on constitutional and administrative law, and to Scott Smith and John Veroneau for their encouragement.

I have always leaned on the superior wisdom of my friends and family, and this book was no exception. Alan Siegel of Siegelvision, one of the nation's leading experts on branding and on simplification, lent judgment and his team to help sort through title difficulties. My downstairs neighbor Sean Brady was a full-service exploitee, offering helpful suggestions on the title, taking my photograph, and reading drafts. Conrad Scott performed his son-in-law duties brilliantly, offering many helpful editorial comments and a few points of useful resistance. Henry Reath as usual came up with just the idea to get the introduction moving. Tony Kiser, John Guare, and Dave Johnson held my hand when needed. Professor Philip Bobbitt was a thoughtful sounding board. Richard Gould lobbed in missives from the Right, as did Scott Drum, to make sure I stayed focused on how stupid the current system really is. Olivia Sabine, Charlotte Howard, Lily Howard Scott, and Alexander Howard were encouraging and formed the core of the focus group in the search for a title. Common Good board member Perry Golkin egged me on, and offered several cre-

ative ideas on how to dislodge the current political duopoly. Jim
O'Shaughnessy, also on the board, is fearless about change, and
opens doors better than anyone I've ever met. A support group
from Taft School intervened in the middle of this project, offering ideas on base closing commissions (Ray Dubois), education
reform (John Merrow), political narratives (Bob Whitcomb),
and the need always to honor the moral high ground (Lance
Odden and Willy MacMullen). Michael Formichelli provided a
philosopher's feedback.

The publishing team from W. W. Norton is first rate. I'm
lucky to have Starling Lawrence as editor, and he and I are
both lucky to work with his assistants, Emma Hitchcock and
Nneoma Amadi-obi. Copy editor Nancy Green kept me reasonably tethered to the English language. My agent Andrew
Wylie is wonderfully purposeful and effective.

Finally, Alexandra encouraged me throughout. It's helpful,
in the middle of fifteen-hour writing days, to have a lovely person repeatedly telling you that what you're doing is important.
Alexandra Cushing Howard is her own invention, and illus-
trates the unique potential of each of us to create a life and a
world that is surprising and good.

NOTES

Introduction

11 **sooner than I expected:** See Philip K. Howard, *The Rule of Nobody* (New York: W. W. Norton, 2014), 144–47.

11 **[working] with the new administration and Congress:** I was a member of President Trump's Strategic Policy Council, advising on how to streamline infrastructure permitting; the council disbanded after the Charlottesville demonstrations. I also testified before Congress on issues related to rebuilding infrastructure and small-business regulation, and worked with congressional and executive branch staff.

14 **Historic shifts:** See Howard, *Rule of Nobody*, 144–47.

15 **a rigid conception of the Rule of Law:** See Howard, *Rule of Nobody*, 26–46.

15 **Waiting for someone else to fill that vacuum is perilous:** Polling shows that Americans, and younger Americans in particular, have soured on the promise of democracy, and are increasingly receptive to undemocratic alternatives. A 2016 paper by Roberto Stefan Foa and Yascha Mounk relates that "when asked to rate on a scale of 1 to 10 how 'essential' it is for them 'to live in a democracy,'" only around 30 percent of millennials responded "10." Foa and Mounk also found: "In the past three decades, the share of U.S. citizens who think that it would be a 'good' or 'very good' thing for the 'army to rule'—a patently undemocratic stance—has steadily risen. In 1995, just one in sixteen respon-

dents agreed with that position; today, one in six agree." "The Danger of Deconsolidation: The Democratic Disconnect," *Journal of Democracy* 27, no. 3 (2016): 7–8, 12. See also Roberto Stefan Foa and Yascha Mounk, "Are Americans Losing Faith in Democracy?," Vox, December 18, 2015.

15 **losing hope of a better future:** A Pew poll from 2017 reports that the "U.S. may be one of the richest countries in the world, with one of the highest per capita gross domestic products among major nations, but Americans are fairly pessimistic about economic prospects for their country's children. Just 37 percent of Americans believe that today's children will grow up to be better off financially than their parents": Bruce Stokes, "Public Divided on Prospects for the Next Generation," Pew Research Center, June 5, 2017.

16 **"old order has ceased to have validity":** Peter F. Drucker, *The End of Economic Man: A Study of the New Totalitarianism,* rev. ed. (Piscataway, NJ: Transaction, 1995), 82: "The old order has ceased to have validity and reality, and its world has therefore become irrational and demonic. But there has emerged no new order which would have brought a new basis of belief, and from which we could develop new forms and new institutions to organize social reality so as to enable us to attain a new supreme goal." Quotations at 14, 104, 210.

16 **"successfully links the dictatorships":** Winston Churchill, review of *The End of Economic Man, Times Literary Supplement,* May 27, 1939.

17 **What Winston Churchill provided:** Drucker, *End of Economic Man,* xxvii.

17 **"Every organized society":** Drucker, *End of Economic Man,* 45.

Part I: Replacing a Failed Philosophy

19 **"The evil of our times":** Karol Wojtyla, Letter to Henri du Lubac, quoted in du Lubac, *At the Service of the Church* (San Francisco: Ignatius Press, 1993), 171–72.

20 **Indian Ladder Farms:** Steve Eder, "When Picking Apples on a Farm With 5,000 Rules, Watch Out for the Ladders," *New York Times,* December 27, 2017; Matt Brown interviews with Peter G. Ten Eyck II, February and July 2018. Many of the regulations are part of a USDA certification program that is supposedly voluntary but effectively

mandatory because they are required by virtually every buyer. The impracticality of some requirements requires adaptive workarounds. For example, the rule about checking for mouse and deer droppings is intended to prevent workers from stepping on them, having their boots spread them to the rungs of the ladder, then getting on the workers' hands as they grasp the rungs, and so forth. Finding it "ridiculous" in practice, the orchard simply instructed employees to grab only the sides of ladders.

20 **donation of a prom dress:** Marc Munroe Dion, "Red Tape Precludes Westport School Committee From Accepting Donated Prom Dress," [Fall River, MA] *Herald News*, April 30, 2011.

21 **two volunteer firefighters:** Vanessa Remmers, "Stafford Firefighters Suspended After Taking Child to Hospital in Fire Engine," [Fredericksburg, VA] *Free Lance-Star*, March 5, 2016.

21 **Reuters compiled a report:** Reade Levinson, "Across the U.S., Police Contracts Shield Officers From Scrutiny and Discipline," Reuters, January 13, 2017.

22 **"zero tolerance" policy for immigrants:** See, e.g., Camila Domonoske and Richard Gonzales, "What We Know: Family Separation and 'Zero Tolerance' at the Border," National Public Radio, June 19, 2018.

22 **"We don't want to separate families":** See, e.g., Ted Hesson, "Trump Administration to Step Up Family Separation at the Border," Politico, May 7, 2018.

22 **"an absence of judgment, institutionalized":** "Should Migration at the Border Be Called a Refugee Crisis?," MTP Daily, MSNBC, June 22, 2018. Will also declared, in the same segment: "Any policy, anywhere, on any subject, at any time, that is based on zero tolerance of X is going to fail. Because the whole point of 'zero tolerance' is to make it unnecessary, indeed impossible, to think, to exercise judgment."

22 **Dr. Colleen Kraft:** Kristine Phillips, " 'America Is Better Than This': What a Doctor Saw in a Texas Shelter for Migrant Children," *Washington Post*, June 16, 2018. A former employee of a New York City shelter where separated children are held told MSNBC: "We're not allowed to know what's going on with the child. We're not allowed to ask any of the kids questions. If the child is not OK, the only thing we're allowed to ask is, 'Do you want to speak to your case manager? Do you want

to speak to your clinician?"' She added: "We're not allowed to hug the kids.... We're not allowed to touch them at all.... I decided not to follow that rule this week. This week I hugged them. I don't care anymore": "Surreptitious Video Offers Peek at Impact of Trump Border Policy," The Rachel Maddow Show, MSNBC, June 25, 2018.

23 **Bloomberg on "management problem":** Exchange by author with Michael Bloomberg, February 2015.

Chapter 1: America the Practical

25 **"The Founding Fathers . . . were extremely pragmatic":** Peter Drucker, *A Functioning Society* (New Brunswick: Transaction, 2003), 20.

26 **America spends more money on schools:** OECD, Education at a Glance 2017: OECD Indicators (Paris: OECD Publishing, 2017), 171.

27 **"The essential condition of responsibility":** Friedrich A. Hayek, *The Constitution of Liberty* (Chicago: University of Chicago Press, 1960), 84.

27 **practicality can't be preset in rules:** See Aristotle, *Nicomachean Ethics* (Oxford: Oxford University Press, 2009), 24: "The whole account of matters of conduct must be given in outline and not precisely . . . the accounts we demand must be in accordance with the subject-matter; matters concerned with conduct and questions of what is good for us have no fixity, any more than matters of health." See generally Michael Polanyi, *Personal Knowledge* (Chicago: University of Chicago Press, 1962); Michael Rose, *The Mind at Work* (New York: Penguin Books, 2004).

28 **"Responsibility, in order to be reasonable":** James Madison, "No. 63," *The Federalist Papers* (New York: Modern Library, 2001), 402.

28 **"The sole and undivided responsibility":** Alexander Hamilton, "No. 76," *The Federalist Papers*, 485.

28 **"shifted from one to another":** Alexander Hamilton, "No. 70," *The Federalist Papers*, 453.

28 **"Whenever one person is found adequate":** George Washington, quoted in Leonard D. White, *The Federalists: A Study in Administrative History* (New York: Macmillan, 1948), 91.

29 **Like deposing an aging dictator:** George Maynard Keynes, *The General Theory of Employment, Interest, and Money* (New York: Harcourt, 1965), vii: "The difficulty lies, not in the new ideas, but in escaping from the old ones."

Chapter 2: The Fixation on Correctness

30 **"The nature of despotic power":** Alexis de Tocqueville, *Democracy in America* (New York; Vintage Books, 1990), 2: 140.

30 **What it touts as major reforms:** See, for example, discussion on the FAST Act (page 73).

31 **it should do with tight controls:** See discussion in Philip K. Howard, *The Rule of Nobody* (New York: W. W. Norton, 2014), 14–20, 26–38, and Howard, *The Death of Common Sense* (New York: Random House, 1995), 22–38.

33 **attributes his unlikely path:** J. D. Vance, *Hillbilly Elegy: A Memoir of a Family and Culture in Crisis* (New York: HarperCollins, 2016), and author conversation, 2017. In order for nonparent relatives to make critical parenting decisions on behalf of children, including school enrollment and consent for medical interventions, formalized legal approvals such as custody or adoption are required. See, e.g., J. Conrad Glass Jr. and Terry L. Huneycutt, "Grandparents Raising Grandchildren: The Courts, Custody, and Educational Implications," *Educational Gerontology* 28, no. 3 (2002): 237–51. See generally www .grandfamilies.org.

33 **the roadway of the Bayonne Bridge:** See Howard, *Rule of Nobody,* 7–12.

33 **The breakdown of schools:** Gerald Grant, *The World We Created at Hamilton High* (Cambridge, MA: Harvard University Press, 1990); Richard Arum, *Judging School Discipline* (Cambridge, MA: Harvard University Press, 2005); Philip W. Jackson, Robert E. Boorstrom, and David T. Hansen, *The Moral Life of Schools* (San Francisco: Jossey-Bass, 1998); Sara Lawrence-Lightfoot, *The Good High School* (New York: Basic Books, 1983).

34 **rationalist tradition of Enlightenment thinkers:** Howard, *Death of Common Sense,* 27–29, 50–53. Voltaire wrote, "Let all the laws be

clear, uniform, and precise; to interpret laws is almost always to corrupt them." Quoted in John R. Howe, *Language and Political Meaning in Revolutionary America* (Amherst: University of Massachusetts Press, 2004), 38.

34 **"Soviet-Harvard delusion":** Nassim Taleb, *Antifragile: Things That Gain from Disorder* (New York: Random House, 2012), 9–10: "The fragilista falls for the *Soviet-Harvard delusion*, the (unscientific) overestimation of the reach of scientific knowledge."

35 **firemen in Washington stood by:** Peter Hermann, "Man, 77, Dies After Collapsing Near D.C. Fire Station and Not Getting Immediate Aid," *Washington Post*, January 29, 2014.

35 **School administrators in New York refused to call 911:** Carrie Melago, "How Queens School Failed Mariya Fatima After Stroke," [New York] *Daily News*, September 10, 2007.

36 **modern government a "vetocracy":** Francis Fukuyama, *Political Order and Political Decay* (New York: Farrar, Straus and Giroux), 488–505.

36 **The political noise is all for show:** See Václav Havel, *The Art of the Impossible* (New York: Knopf, 1997), 126. "Politicians seem to have turned into puppets that only look human and move in a giant, rather inhuman theatre; they appear to have become merely cogs in a huge machine, objects of a major automatism of civilization which has gotten out of control and for which no one is responsible."

Chapter 3: Back to Basics: Allocate Scope of Responsibility

37 **"A free society rests":** Peter Drucker, *The Age of Discontinuity* (New York: Harper & Row, 1968), 258: "But this *freedom from* the abuse of power is not enough for a free society. A free society rests on the *freedom to* make responsible decisions."

37 **"find ourselves at the mercy":** Philip Slater, *The Pursuit of Loneliness: American Culture at the Breaking Point* (Boston: Beacon Press, 1990), 158.

38 **"Power is one of those rare commodities":** William J. O'Brien, *The Soul of Corporate Leadership: Guidelines for Values-Centered Governance* (Waltham, MA: Pegasus Communications, 1998). See discus-

sion in Philip K. Howard, *The Rule of Nobody* (New York: W. W. Norton, 2014), 114–16: "Authority, properly understood, dramatically expands freedom," and Howard, *The Collapse of Common Good* (New York: Ballantine, 2002), 144–55.

39 **conflict is sown in human nature:** See James Madison, "Liberty is to faction what air is to fire, an aliment without which it instantly expires. But it could not be less folly to abolish liberty, which is essential to political life, because it nourishes faction, than it would be to wish the annihilation of air, which is essential to animal life, because it imparts to fire its destructive agency": Madison, "No. 10," *The Federalist Papers* (New York: Modern Library, 2001), 54–55.

39 **"safety valve":** Lewis Coser, *The Functions of Social Conflict* (New York: Free Press, 1964), 39-41. See also Peter Drucker, *The Essential Drucker* (New York: HarperCollins, 2001), 254: "Develop Disagreement. Unless one has considered alternatives, one has a closed mind.... The first rule in decision-making is that one does not make a decision unless there is disagreement." A core management principle that Amazon founder Jeff Bezos has emblazoned on the walls of its facilities is "Disagree and Commit": Justin Bariso, "In Just 3 Words, Amazon's Jeff Bezos Taught a Brilliant Lesson in Leadership," *Inc.* Magazine (April 13, 2017).

39 **Even when people don't get their way:** Jeremy Waldron, "The Concept and the Rule of Law," *Georgia Law Review* 43, no. 1 (Fall 2008): 23: "A mode of governing people that treats them with respect," Waldron explains, requires allowing them to present "a view of their own to present on the application of a norm to their conduct or situation."

39 **rigid systems:** Coser, *Functions of Social Conflict*, 154.

39 **"[keep] the small rules":** George Orwell, *1984* (New York: Harcourt, 1983), 123.

39 **"tear apart":** Coser, *Functions of Social Conflict*, 157.

39 **"The greatest menace to freedom":** Justice Louis Brandeis, *Whitney v. California*, 274 US 357, 375 (1927).

40 **the Erie Canal:** "Clinton's big ditch": www.eriecanal.org.

41 **"The idea of law":** Grant Gilmore, *The Ages of American Law*, 2d ed. (New Haven: Yale University Press, 2014), 94. See also introduc-

tion by Philip Bobbitt, 124–49. Henry Steele Commager identified the tendency as "an almost lawless passion for lawmaking" in *The American Mind* (New Haven: Yale University Press, 1959), 363.

42 **"official's discretion":** Ronald Dworkin, *Taking Rights Seriously* (Cambridge, MA: Harvard University Press, 1978), 31. Václav Havel observed that there's no reason to fear giving a person authority if there is accountability "when a person betrays that responsibility": Havel, *The Art of the Impossible* (New York: Knopf, 1997), 201.

Chapter 4: How Correctness Causes Failure and Alienation

43 **"Nothing that's any good":** Neil Baldwin, *Edison* (Chicago: University of Chicago Press, 2001), 296.

43 **"mightily addicted to rules":** David Hume, *A Treatise of Human Nature*, L. A. Selby-Bigge and P. H. Nidditch, eds. (Oxford: Oxford University Press, 1978), 551. "This passion for bureaucracy," sociologist Max Weber said, "is enough to drive one to despair," quoted in J. P. Mayer, *Max Weber and German Politics* (London: Faber, 1944),125–31. See also Friedrich A. Hayek, *The Road to Serfdom* (Chicago: University of Chicago Press, 2007), 114: our age has a "passion for conscious control of everything."

43 **people demand conflicting rights:** See Philip K. Howard, *The Death of Common Sense* (New York: Random House, 1995), 115–71.

44 **kaleidoscope of situations:** See Michael Polanyi, *Personal Knowledge* (Chicago: University of Chicago Press, 1962), 79: "The world, like a kaleidoscope, never exactly repeats any prior situation."

44 **The truth of any matter:** This concept is attributed to nineteenth-century historian Henry Thomas Buckle by Charles and Mary Beard. Nassim Taleb makes a similar point in *Antifragile: Things That Gain from Disorder* (New York: Random House, 2012), 248: "I still have the instinct that the treasure, what one needs to know for a profession, is necessarily what lies outside the corpus, as far away from the center as possible."

44 **"rarely a choice between right and wrong":** Drucker, *The Essential Drucker* (New York: HarperCollins, 2001), 251.

44 **they're wearing blinders:** See Taleb, *Antifragile*, 194–97; "We need

to learn to think in second steps, chains of consequences, and side effects," 107, and "We just cannot isolate any causal relationship in a complex system," 58. See also Jerry Z. Muller, *The Tyranny of Metrics* (Princeton: Princeton University Press, 2018), 59–64.

44 **Spending years preparing:** See Philip K. Howard, "Two Years Not Ten Years" (New York: Common Good, 2015).

45 **It depends on the situation:** Isaiah Berlin, *The Crooked Timber of Humanity: Chapters in the History of Ideas*, ed. Henry Hardy (Princeton: Princeton University Press, 2013), 19: "The concrete situation is almost everything."

45 **the janitor cleaned the room again:** Barry Schwartz and Kenneth Sharpe, *Practical Wisdom: The Right Way to Do the Right Thing* (New York: Riverhead Books, 2010), 13–17.

45 **people with lobotomies:** Antonio Damasio, *Descartes' Error* (New York: Penguin, 1994), 35–51, 245–52.

46 **"usual process of unconscious trial and error":** Polanyi, *Personal Knowledge,* 62.

46 **"tacit knowledge":** Polanyi, *Personal Knowledge,* 92.

46 **People get so immersed in a project:** See Gary Klein, *Intuition at Work: Why Developing Your Gut Instinct Will Make You Better at What You Do* (New York: Currency, 2004).

46 **They *become* the project:** In describing the "miracle on the Hudson," when airline pilot "Sully" Sullenberger successfully glided an airliner with no power to a safe crash landing on the Hudson River, William Langewiesche writes that "across a lifetime of flying, Sullenberger had developed an intimacy with these machines that is difficult to convey. He did not sit in airplanes as much as put them on." Langewiesche, *Fly By Wire* (New York: Farrar, Straus and Giroux, 2009), 177. Sullenberger himself described the final moments this way: "The earth and the river were rushing toward us. I was judging the descent rate and our altitude visually. At that instant, I judged it was the right time. I began the flare for landing. I pulled the side stick back, farther back, finally full aft, and held it there as we touched the water": Sullenberger, "What I Got Back," *Parade*, October 11, 2009.

47 **"I don't know who writes it":** Author conversation with Henry Stern, 2014.

47 **Doing anything successfully:** Polanyi, *Personal Knowledge,* 127: "Obsession with one's problem is in fact the mainspring of all inventive power."

47 **Philip Jackson's study of successful teachers:** See generally Jackson, Boorstrom, and Hansen, *The Moral Life of Schools* (San Francisco: Jossey-Bass, 1998).

47 **"You need not see what someone is doing":** W. H. Auden, "Horae Canonicae," in *Selected Poems,* ed. Edward Mendelson (New York: Vintage, 2007), 227.

47 **"call for sensitive observation and judgment":** Michael Lipsky, *Street-Level Bureaucracy* (New York: Russell Sage 2010), 15. See Jeremy Waldron, *Nonsense Upon Stilts* (London: Routledge, 1987), 91–92: "The wise man sees or feels what is to be done," Waldron observes (channeling Edmund Burke), "rather than trying consciously to work it out."

47 **"guided discretion":** See introduction by Philip Howard to Herbert Kaufman, *Red Tape* (Washington: Brookings Institution Press, 2015), xiii–xvii; Herbert Kaufman, *The Forest Ranger* (London: Routledge Press, 2006).

47 **Worker safety was enhanced in Maine:** See US Department of Labor, Occupational Safety and Health Administration, *Reflections on OSHA's History,* OSHA 3360 (Washington, DC: OSHA, 2009), 39–40.

47 **goals-displacement:** See Muller, *Tyranny of Metrics,* 169–73.

48 **Surgeons who were evaluated by mortality rate:** Muller, *Tyranny of Metrics,* 117–18, provides ample evidence supporting what is known as "Campbell's Law" ("The more any quantitative social indicator is used for social decision-making, . . . the more apt it will be to distort and corrupt the social processes it is intended to monitor": quoting Donald T. Campbell, 19.)

48 **an experiment asking people to count:** Daniel J. Simons, "Selective Attention Test," YouTube, March 10, 2010.

48 ***not* justifying each step:** See Malcolm Gladwell, *Blink: The Power of Thinking without Thinking* (Boston: Back Bay Books, 2007), 179–81. A study on consumer ability to discern popular taste in jam found that the group required to explain their reasons made worse choices than those who simply made a judgment without reasons.

48 **"Too much reliance on rules":** Schwartz and Sharpe, *Practical Wis-*

dom, 41–42: "Psychologist Karl Weick found that traditionally, successful firefighters kept four simple survival guidelines in mind.... But starting in the mid-1950s, this short list of survival rules was gradually replaced by much longer and more detailed ones... teaching the firefighters these detailed lists was a factor in decreasing the survival rates." Thomas Edison provides a pithy statement of the conflict between rules and accomplishment: "Hell! There ain't no rules around here! We are tryin' to accomplish somep'n." See Baldwin, *Edison,* 296.

49 **Working is about the search:** Studs Terkel, *Working* (New York: New Press, 1997), ix. See also Samuel Fleischacker, *A Third Concept of Liberty* (Princeton: Princeton University Press, 1999), 93: "We spend much of our lives setting ourselves small tasks and we live, much of the time, for the pleasures of completing these tasks successfully. In each of these tasks we want a problem to solve, on which we can exercise our judgment.... What makes these tasks interesting is that they demand good judgment. If the problems... can be solved merely 'mechanically,'... then completion of the task brings no pleasure."

49 **"flow" of accomplishing things:** See Mihaly Csikszentmihaly, *Flow* (New York: Harper Perennial, 2008).

49 **People are energized:** Daniel Pink, *Drive* (New York: Riverhead Books 2009), 68–79; Edward Deci, *Why We Do What We Do* (New York: Penguin Books 1996).

49 **"Few things help an individual more":** Booker T. Washington, *Up from Slavery* (New York: Doubleday, Page, 1907), 172.

49 **Constant justification:** Eugene Bardach and Robert Kagan, *Going by the Book* (New York: Transaction, 2002), 28–29, 90–91.

49 **"lack of control":** Professor Christina Maslach, a leading researcher on the cause of "burnout," has identified six "mismatches" that can bring it about. In addition to lack of control, they include other bureaucracy-produced conditions like "breakdown of community" and "conflicting values." Only one of the mismatches includes the amount of work: John Rampton, "The 6 Causes of Professional Burnout and How to Avoid Them," Forbes.com, May 13, 2015. See Christina Maslach and Michael P. Leiter, *The Truth About Burnout: How Organizations Cause Personal Stress and What to Do About It* (San Francisco:

Jossey-Bass, 1997); Cary Cherniss, *Professional Burnout in Human Service Organizations* (Westport, CT: Praeger, 1980), notes that burnout is often "caused by emotional drain due to routine, monotony, and lack of control"; Wilmar B. Schaufeli, Christina Maslach, and Tadeusz Marek, eds., *Professional Burnout: Recent Developments in Theory and Research* (Washington, DC: Taylor & Francis, 1993), 132. The first listed cause of "burnout" by the Mayo Clinic is "lack of control." Mayo Clinic, "Job Burnout: How to Spot It and Take Action," http://www.mayoclinic.com/health/burnout/WL00062. See also Eric Garton, "Employee Burnout Is a Problem with the Company, Not the Person," *Harvard Business Review*, April 6, 2017: "One of the greatest sources of organizational energy is giving employees a sense of autonomy."

Chapter 5: Forty Years of Marginal Reforms

50 **"Nothing makes conditions more unbearable":** Friedrich A. Hayek, *The Road to Serfdom* (Chicago: University of Chicago Press, 2007), 128.

50 **The philosophy of correctness was born:** See Philip K. Howard, *The Rule of Nobody* (New York: W. W. Norton, 2014), 104–10, and *The Death of Common Sense* (New York: Random House, 1995), 24–31.

51 **expanded the coverage of "due process":** See Philip K. Howard, "History of American Law since 1968," in *Oxford Companion to American Law*, ed. Kermit L. Hall (New York: Oxford University Press, 2002), 393–96.

51 **seven pages of rules on ladders:** See generally 29 CFR §1910.23 and 29 CFR §1926.1053; see also U.S. Department of Labor, Occupational Safety and Health Administration, "Stairways and Ladders: A Guide to OSHA Rules," OSHA 3124-12R (Washington, DC: OSHA, 2003).

51 **to threaten schools with claims:** See Philip K. Howard, *Life Without Lawyers* (New York: W. W. Norton, 2009), 52–53, 62–64.

51 **"crisis of the most serious magnitude":** Quoted in Robert Nisbet, *Twilight of Authority* (Carmel, IN: Liberty Fund, 2000), 11.

52 **"to reorganize a Federal Government":** Jimmy Carter, "Improving Government Regulations Statement on Executive Order 12044," March 23, 1978.

52 **ideas from [Carter's] domestic policy adviser:** See generally Stuart E. Eizenstat, *President Carter: The White House Years* (New York: St. Martin's Press, 2018).

52 **"Too many Federal programs":** Jimmy Carter: "Sunset Review Legislation Statement by the President," The American Presidency Project, May 23, 1979.

52 **"government is not the solution":** Ronald Reagan, Inaugural Address, The American Presidency Project, January 20, 1981.

52 **the Grace Commission:** See Thomas M. Hill, "Trump's 1st State of the Union: Will He Have a Plan to Reform the 'Deep State?'" Brookings Institution, January 24, 2018.

53 **"a problem that's been 40 years in the making":** Ronald Reagan, "Remarks at a White House Luncheon for the Chairman and Executive Committee of the Private Sector Survey on Cost Control in the Federal Government," March 10, 1982.

53 **"base closing commissions":** See Hill, "Trump's 1st State of the Union," Brookings Institution, January 24, 2018; George Schlossberg, "How Congress Cleared the Bases: A Legislative History of BRAC," *Journal of Defense Communities* 1 (2012).

53 **Gore's "reinventing government":** See Al Gore, *Common Sense Government: Works Better and Costs Less,* introduction by Philip K. Howard (New York: Random House, 1995), xxiv, 39–43.

54 **George W. Bush proposed a tort reform bill:** Personal interactions of author with senior staff of the White House; Howard, *Rule of Nobody,* 138.

54 **Barack Obama was the freshest face:** Compare Cass Sunstein, *Simpler: The Future of Government* (New York: Simon & Schuster 2014), *passim* (generally supporting more flexibility), with Sunstein, "Problems with Rules," *California Law Review* 83, no. 4 (July 1995): 1022: "Frequently a lawmaker adopts rules because rules narrow or even eliminate the range of disagreement and uncertainty faced by people attempting to follow or to interpret the law. This step has enormous virtues in terms of promoting predictability and planning and reducing both costs and risks of official abuse."

54 **"I must have missed that":** Author conversation with Ron Faucheux. Commenting on the limited scope of regulatory reform under Obama,

liberal columnist Joe Klein notes, "His people can tell you the number of unnecessary regulations they've eliminated. It barely scratches the surface of what needs to be done—there is no creative destruction in government, regulations pile up on top of each other like silt, generation after generation." Klein, "More Brill, More Obamacare Incompetence," In the Arena (blog), April 4, 2013. See William H. Simon, "The Republic of Choosing: A Behaviorist Goes to Washington" (review of *Simpler: The Future of Government*), *Boston Review*, July 8, 2013.

54 **eight million Obama supporters turned around:** A June 2017 analysis by the University of Virginia Center for Politics looked at three different data sources and found that the number of Obama-Trump voters totaled an estimated 6.7 million, 8.4 million, or 9.2 million. Geoffrey Skelley, "Just How Many Obama 2012-Trump 2016 Voters Were There?," Sabato's Crystal Ball, June 1, 2017.

Chapter 6: Unworkable Political Ideologies

57 **"The insistence . . . on a 'rationally perfect' law":** Peter Drucker, *A Functioning Society: Community, Society, and Polity in the Twentieth Century* (New Brunswick: Transaction, 2003), 7–8.

59 **price gouging was the best way to allocate scarce water supplies:** See Andrew Ross Sorkin, "Hurricane Price Gouging is Despicable, Right? Not to Some Economists," *New York Times*, September 11, 2017.

59 **Hayek specifically used the example of water shortage:** Friedrich A. Hayek, *The Constitution of Liberty* (Chicago: University of Chicago, 1960), 136: "A monopolist could exercise true coercion, however, if he were, say, the owner of a spring in an oasis. Let us say that other persons settled there on the assumption that water would always be available at a reasonable price and then found, perhaps because a second spring dried up, that they had no choice but to do whatever the owner of the spring demanded of them if they were to survive: here would be a clear case of coercion."

59 **the patron saint for libertarians:** See Angus Burgin, *The Great Persuasion* (Cambridge, MA: Harvard University Press, 2015), 178: "I wish I was as sure of one thing as Milton Friedman is of all things" (relating a conversation with Robert McKenzie); 202–3 on civil rights:

"He believed that the market, over time and aided by continued public discussion, would eventually lead people to act as the advocates of civil rights legislation wished." Following his profile of Friedman in *Fortune*, journalist John Davenport concluded that business had "abandoned a language of values," begin at 209.

60 **"Man exists for his own sake":** Ayn Rand, *The Virtue of Selfishness* (New York: Signet, 1964), 23.

60 **"self-interest, rightly understood":** Alexis de Tocqueville, *Democracy in America* (New York: Vintage, 1990), 1: 393.

60 **Most libertarians readily acknowledge:** See generally Reason. com, for a thoughtful compendium of libertarian thought.

61 **"first duty [of] public officials":** Barry Goldwater, *Conscience of a Conservative* (Radford VA: Wilder Publications, 2009), 13.

61 **Eric Foner:** *The Story of American Freedom* (New York: W. W. Norton, 1998), 310 (quoting conservative historian Clinton Rossiter).

61 **No citizen or business, not even a corporation:** See Philip K. Howard, *The Death of Common Sense* (New York: Random House, 1995), 31–33.

61 **curb the evil of judicial activism:** See Philip K. Howard, *Life Without Lawyers* (New York: W. W. Norton, 2009), 85–86.

62 **"I don't want to abolish government":** Grover Norquist, interview with Mara Liasson, National Public Radio, May 25, 2001.

63 **Mario Cuomo bridge:** Author conversation with Robert Yaro at Regional Plan Authority, 2015.

63 **"simultaneous recession of both freedom and authority":** Hannah Arendt, "What is Authority?" in Arendt, *Between Past and Future* (New York: Penguin, 1977), 100.

65 **economist Joseph Stiglitz:** Stiglitz, *The Price of Inequality* (New York: W. W. Norton, 2013), 18, 117 (referring to a "long-term underinvestment in public education").

65 **Environmental review should be preserved:** See, e.g., Daniel C. Vock, "To Speed Up Infrastructure Projects, Trump Revisits Environmental Regs," *Governing*, March 13, 2017. The Center for American Progress characterized Common Good's "Two Years, Not Ten Years" report as an attack on the idea of environmental review by "hardcore opponents of environmental review." Common Good, "Red Tape, Not

Progress: The Center for American Progress Defends Bureaucratic Paralysis," June 2017, https://www.commongood.org/?s=center+for+american+progress. See George Will, "How we waste a massive amount of infrastructure money—before building even starts," *Washington Post*, June 9, 2017.

65 **The Democratic platform is almost completely devoid:** Democratic Platform Committee, "2016 Democratic Party Platform," July 2016.

66 **liberal professor Mark Lilla:** Lilla, *The Once and Future Liberal* (New York: HarperCollins, 2017), 9–10. "The main result has been to turn young people back onto themselves, rather than turning them outward toward the wider world. It has left them unprepared to think about the common good and what must be done practically to secure it—especially the hard and unglamorous task of persuading people very different from themselves to join a common effort."

66 **A new drug may save the lives of thousands:** See generally Cass Sunstein, *Risk and Reason: Safety, Law, and the Environment* (Chicago: University of Chicago Press, 2002).

67 **Campaign funding is sleazy:** See Lawrence Lessig, *Republic, Lost: How Money Corrupts Congress—and a Plan to Stop It* (New York: Hachette, 2011). Lessig proposes small-dollar public funding as a way to limit the influence of campaign contributions from corporations and unions. See also Robert G. Kaiser, *So Damn Much Money: The Triumph of Lobbying and the Corrosion of American Government* (New York: Alfred A. Knopf, 2009).

67 **Gerrymandering to create "safe seats":** See David Daley, *Ratf**ked: Why Your Vote Doesn't Count* (New York: W. W. Norton, 2016), xxvii. "When districts are uncompetitive and weighted to advantage one party, the only election that matters is the party primary, which means the only pressure on the majority of our elected representatives—the Republicans, in other words—comes from a sliver of the far right."

67 **"perfect law code":** Drucker, *A Functioning Society*, 8, 71, 75, 80.

68 **as the Progressive Movement was:** Michael McGerr, *A Fierce Discontent: The Rise and Fall of the Progressive Movement in America* (Oxford: Oxford University Press, 1995).

68 **"get the right things done":** Drucker, *A Functioning Society*, 101.

Chapter 7: Give Responsibility to Identifiable People

71 **"Responsibility, to be effective"**: Friedrich A. Hayek, *The Constitution of Liberty* (Chicago: University of Chicago, 1960), 83.

71 **"a principle of management"**: Peter Drucker, *Management,* rev. ed. (New York: Collins, 2008), 267.

72 **Management theories and structures succeed only as tools:** See Adrian Wooldridge, *Masters of Management* (New York: Harper Business, 2011). Wooldridge argues that management theories contradict each other. I think contradiction may be their main virtue, by providing people different perspectives on what's important. Organizations are too complex, too *human*, to be squeezed through a single filter. By itself, each management theory fails:

- The "scientific management" expounded by Frederick Winslow Taylor improved efficiency in assembly line settings... until it so deadened the human spirit that quality declined. See Philip K. Howard, *Collapse of the Common Good* (New York: Ballantine, 2002), 83–94.

- Evaluating employees by metrics engages their creativity... but only to meet the metrics; in their quest for short-term profits, or higher test scores, they end up undermining the institution's ultimate goal. See generally Jerry Z. Muller, *The Tyranny of Metrics* (Princeton: Princeton University Press, 2018).

- Using information technology to impose Tayloristic methods and second-by-second monitoring, as Simon Head has described, allows electronic surveillance unimaginable even to Orwell... until it causes people to burn out. See Simon Head, *Mindless* (New York: Basic Books, 2014).

- Trying to avoid human bias in government by neutral processes, as I describe in *The Death of Common Sense* (New York: Random House, 1995), 57–111, avoids unfairness by... avoiding decisions altogether. The buck never stops.

- New bureaucracies, such as a sixteen-agency infrastructure permitting council, are created to manage old bureaucracies... until they need another new bureaucracy to manage themselves. See discussion at page 73.

None of these theories is completely wrong, but they won't work except as implemented by humans exercising judgment in ways that, often, contradict the theory. The choices needed to make an institution work, and to provide a work culture in which people flourish, are too varied, values-laden, and fact-dependent to be organized like a machine.

72 **"particular decisions without having to ask"**: Jonathan Wallace, "Leadership," www.spectacle.org, October 1998.

73 **"Two Years, Not Ten Years"**: Philip K. Howard, "Two Years, Not Ten Years: Redesigning Infrastructure Approvals" (New York: Common Good, 2015), www.commongood.org.

73 **sixteen-agency council**: FAST Act, Pub. L. 114-94 (December 4, 2015).

73 **"If a dispute remains unresolved"**: FAST Act at Sec. 41003(c)(2)(B)(ii).

73 **"How long will it take to schedule"**: Author meeting with White House officials, 2016.

74 **"Liberty means responsibility"**: George Bernard Shaw, *Man and Superman* (New York: Penguin Classics, 2001), 251.

74 **the security of an authoritarian system**: Erich Fromm, *Escape from Freedom* (New York: Holt, 1994), 78–79

74 **"near-total preoccupation"**: Charles Peters, *How Washington Really Works* (New York: Basic Books, 1992), 43.

74 **"the resulting system . . . is practically indestructible"**: Max Weber, *Economy and Society,* trans. G. Roth and C. Wittich (New York: Bedminster Press, 1968), 987.

75 **"want to be elected"**: Associated Press, "Bumpers Named Arkansan of the Year," [Mountain Home, AR] *Baxter Bulletin*, August 18, 1998.

75 **Jim Cooper**: Interview by author with Jim Cooper, May 2018.

75 **"clear law"**: See William Voegeli, "Why Corporations Love Regulation," *Commentary*, June 1, 2011: "The political power vested in interventionist government bureaucracies responds to those most adept at exerting pressure and making appeals . . . [like] cunning corporatists who have learned how best to game the system and use it to their advantage"; and Simeon Djankov, *The Regulation of Entry: A Survey,* World Bank International Bank for Reconstruction and Development, May 2009, arguing that stricter, more compliance-oriented business registration regimes primarily benefit incumbents by creating heavy barriers to entry.

75 **Paul Volcker himself thought:** Author lunch with Paul Volcker, 2014.

76 **"feared paternal government":** John Plamenatz, "Liberalism," in *Dictionary of the History of Ideas* (Scribners, 1973), 3: 49.

77 **Fear of authority:** Thomas Hobbes, *Leviathan*, ed. E. M. Curley (Indianapolis, IN: Hackett, 1994), 77: "It may be perceived what manner of life there would be, where there were no common Power to feare."

77 **repudiated without regret:** See John F. Kennedy, "Commencement Address at Yale University," The American Presidency Project, June 11, 1962: "The great enemy of the truth is very often not the lie . . . but the myth—persistent, persuasive, and unrealistic. Too often we hold fast to the clichés of our forebears." See Philip K. Howard, *The Rule of Nobody* (New York: W. W. Norton, 2014), 26–46, 62–74, 110–20.

78 **"The end of law is not to . . . restrain":** John Locke, *The Second Treatise on Civil Government* (Amherst, MA: Prometheus, 1986), 33.

78 **"In their zeal to create":** Isaiah Berlin, *Four Essays on Liberty* (Oxford: Oxford University Press, 1969), liv.

79 **"frontiers, not artificially drawn":** Isaiah Berlin, "Two Concepts of Liberty," *The Proper Study of Mankind: An Anthology of Essays* (New York: Farrar, Straus and Giroux, 2000), 236.

79 **Even brilliant thinkers:** See Howard, *Rule of Nobody*, 29.

79 **deciding what is bad behavior:** See generally Michael Lipsky, *Street-Level Bureaucracy* (New York: Russell Sage, 2010), 15.

80 **"Justice . . . is a concept by far more subtle":** Justice Benjamin Cardozo, *The Growth of the Law* (New Haven; Yale University Press, 1924), 87. See also Aharon Barak (former president of the Israel Supreme Court), *Judicial Discretion*, trans. Yadin Kaufmann (New Haven: Yale University Press, 1989), 261: "Law without discretion ultimately yields arbitrariness."

80 **"zero tolerance" rules:** Philip K. Howard, "Scrap Zero Tolerance Rules," Huffington Post, March 31, 2014.

80 **law hems in the range of action:** Ronald M. Dworkin, *Taking Rights Seriously* (Cambridge, MA: Harvard University Press, 1978), 31, 33: "Discretion, like the hole in a doughnut, does not exist except as an area left open by a surrounding belt of restriction" and "An official's discretion means not that he is free to decide without recourse to standards of sense and fairness."

81 **meant to be applied with common sense and prevailing norms:**
Professor Ofer Raban explains that "indeterminate legal standards
often produce more certainty and predictability than any alternative
bright-line rule because they replicate, one for one, the social, moral,
economic or political norm that already prevails, and which . . . cannot
be reduced to clear and unambiguous language": Raban, "The Fallacy of Legal Certainty: Why Vague Legal Standards May Be Better
for Capitalism and Liberalism," *Boston University Public Interest Law
Journal* 19, no. 2 (Spring 2010): 175–91.

81 **Law is a human institution:** See Howard, *Rule of Nobody*, 72–74. See
also Jeremy Waldron, "The Rule of Law and the Importance of Procedure," in *Getting to the Rule of Law, Nomos 50* (New York: New York
University Press, 2011), 25: "The Rule of Law is, in the end . . . a human
ideal for human institutions, not a magic that somehow absolves us
from human rule."

82 **"For myself, when I feel the hand of power":** Alexis de Tocqueville,
Democracy in America (New York: Vintage, 1990), 2: 12.

83 **rulebooks for nursing homes:** John and Valerie Braithwaite, "The
Politics of Legalism: Rules versus Standards in Nursing-Home Reg-
ulation," *Social and Legal Studies* 4 (1995): 307–41. See discussion in
Howard, *Rule of Nobody*, 47–49.

83 **a legislative proposal to streamline infrastructure red tape:** See
Common Good, "Accelerate Infrastructure Permitting," March 2017,
www.commongood.org.

84 **Guidelines discouraging children from running around and
exploring on their own are counterproductive:** See e.g., Hanna
Rosin, "The Overprotected Kid," *Atlantic*, April 2014; Ellen Barry
March, "In Britain's Playgrounds, 'Bringing in Risk' to Build Resil-
ience," *New York Times*, March 10, 2018; Andrea Petersen, "The Over-
protected American Child," *Wall Street Journal*, June 1, 2018; Lenore
Skenazy, *Free-Range Kids, How to Raise Safe, Self-Reliant Children
(Without Going Nuts with Worry)* (San Francisco: Jossey-Bass, 2010);
Richard Louv, *Last Child in the Woods: Saving Our Children From
Nature-Deficit Disorder* (Chapel Hill, NC: Algonquin Books, 2008);
Hara Estroff Marano, *A Nation of Wimps: The High Cost of Invasive Par-
enting* (New York: Crown Archetype, 2008); Tim Gill, *No Fear: Growing*

Up in a Risk-Averse Society (London: Calouste Gulbenkian Foundation, 2007); Philip K. Howard, *Life Without Lawyers* (New York: W. W. Norton, 2009), 34–48.

84 **It's hard to be streetwise:** See Frank Furedi, *The Culture of Fear Revisited* (London: Continuum, 2006), 123.

84 **The seminal essay:** Aaron Wildavsky, *Searching for Safety* (New Brunswick: Transaction Publishers, 1988), 205–28.

84 **"No plan... survives contact with the enemy":** Helmuth von Moltke the Elder, quoted in *Moltke on the Art of War: Selected Writings,* ed. Daniel J. Hughes (New York: Presidio Press, 1993), vii.

Chapter 8: Restore Accountability to Public Culture

85 **"How can one expect rational administration":** Polybius, *The Histories,* trans. Mortimer Chambers (New York: Washington Square Press, 1966), 226.

85 **"When men are allowed to act":** Friedrich A. Hayek, *The Constitution of Liberty* (Chicago: University of Chicago, 1960), 76.

86 **More federal employees die on the job:** See, e.g., Dennis Cauchon, "Some Federal Workers More Likely to Die Than Lose Jobs," *USA Today,* July 19, 2011.

86 **In California, an average of only two:** *Vergara v. State, et al.*, 202 Cal. Rptr. 3d 262 (2016). See also George F. Will, "The Injustice of California's Teacher Tenure," *Washington Post,* July 13, 2016.

86 **"replacing the bottom 8 percent":** Eric A. Hanushek, "The economic value of higher teacher quality," *Economics of Education Review* 30 (2011): 475.

87 **no one talks about protecting the rights of institutions:** Thoughtful observers of modern society have focused on the decline of local institutions needed for people to be able to act jointly but without emphasizing the authority needed by people within those institutions. See Robert Putnam, *Bowling Alone* (New York: Simon & Schuster, 2001); Yuval Levin, *The Fractured Republic* (New York: Basic Books, 2016).

88 **"objective mechanisms":** Robert N. Bellah et al., *The Good Society* (New York: Vintage Books, 1992), 12.

89 **not mainly the formal structures but the informal ones:** Ches-

ter Barnard, *The Functions of the Executive* (Cambridge, MA: Harvard University Press, 1968), 120–21: "An important and often indispensable part of a formal system of cooperation is informal." See also James Scott, *Seeing Like a State* (New Haven: Yale University Press, 1999), 310: "Formal order . . . is always and to some considerable degree parasitic on informal processes."

89 **"abilities do not exist independent of the environment":** Chester Barnard, quoted in Andrea Gabor, *The Capitalist Philosophers* (New York: Crown Business, 2000), 81. See David Hume, *An Enquiry Concerning Human Understanding* (New York: Barnes & Noble, 2004), 68. "The mutual dependence of men is so great in all societies that scarce any human action is . . . complete in itself."

89 **"The feeling that you are part of a team":** Dennis Bakke, *Joy at Work* (Seattle: Pear Press, 2006), 75.

89 **"No one has a greater asset for his business":** Pauline Graham (ed.), *Mary Parker Follett, Prophet of Management* (District of Columbia: Beard Books, 2003), 126. Mary Follett, born in 1868, was an important thinker in the development of management theory, particularly for her emphasis on "soft" factors such as communications and camaraderie.

90 **22 million Americans work in the public sector:** U.S. Department of Labor, Bureau of Labor Statistics, Economic News Release, Table B-1, as of July 6, 2018.

90 **a sense of ownership:** See Samuel Fleischacker, *A Third Concept of Liberty* (Princeton: Princeton University Press, 1999), 275. Institutions work better where people feel their "institutions are both open to easy change and responsive to the judgments of those they affect."

90 **"A social organism of any sort":** William James, "The Will to Believe," *Pragmatism and Other Writings* (New York: Penguin Classics, 2000), 214.

90 **What accountability does:** See Russell Hardin, "Conceptions and Explanations of Trust," in *Trust in Society*, ed. Karen Cook (New York: Russell Sage, 2001), 4–5, 16–24.

91 **"When a single individual free rides":** X. P. Chen and D. G. Bachrach, "Tolerance of free-riding: The effects of defection size, defection pattern, and social orientation in a repeated public goods dilemma,"

Organizational Behavior and Human Decision Processes 90(1) (2003): 139–147, as described in Will Felps, Terrence R. Mitchell, and Eliza Byington, "How, When, and Why Bad Apples Spoil the Barrel: Negative Group Members and Dysfunctional Groups," *Research in Organizational Behavior* 27: *An Annual Series of Analytical Essays and Critical Reviews,* ed. Barry Staw (Oxford: Elsevier, 2006), 190, 194.

91 **One "bad apple":** Felps, Mitchell, and Byington, "How, When, and Why," 190.

91 **caused educators to resort to cheating:** See Jerry Z. Muller, *The Tyranny of Metrics* (Princeton: Princeton University Press, 2018), 92– 93. John Merrow calls this "edugenesis" in *Addicted to Reform: A 12-Step Program to Rescue Public Education* (New York: New Press, 2017), 61: "All this cheating—by a *minority* of principals and teachers—was the direct result of school reform's intense pressure to raise scores on standardized tests, and threats of dire consequences if scores did not go up."

91 **the work as a "calling":** Amy Wrzesniewski, "Finding Positive Meaning in Work," in *Positive Organizational Scholarship: Foundations of a New Discipline,* ed. Kim S. Cameron, Jane E. Dutton, and Robert E. Quinn (San Francisco: Berrett-Koehler, 2003).

91 **"The question of personal compatibility":** Barnard, *Functions of the Executive,* 146.

92 **"Laying aside all exceptions":** Philip Jackson, Robert E. Boorstrom, and David T. Hansen, *The Moral Life of Schools* (San Francisco: Jossey-Bass, 1998), 34.

92 **Americans on average change jobs ten times:** Remarks by U.S. Secretary of Labor Elaine L. Chao, National Summit on Retirement Savings, Washington, DC, March 1, 2006.

93 **"There have to be people who make decisions":** Peter Drucker, *A Functioning Society: Community, Society, and Polity in the Twentieth Century* (New Brunswick: Transaction, 2003), 122.

93 **"just a matter of due process":** See, e.g., Randi Weingarten, letter to the editor, *New York Observer,* November 20, 2007; Amita Sharma, "Tenure: A Two-Edged Sword for 80 Years," [Riverside, CA] *Press-Enterprise,* April 7, 1999.

93 **"I'm here to defend even the worst":** Allison Pries, "Teacher Union

President Suspended After Allegedly Saying 'I'm Here to Defend Even the Worst People,'" NJ.com, May 2, 2018.

93 **Los Angeles spent five years:** Beth Barrett, "LAUSD's Dance of the Lemons," *LA Weekly*, February 11, 2010.

93 **the EPA employee who spent the day:** Charles S. Clark, "Lawmakers Wonder 'How Much Porn' It Takes to Fire an EPA Employee," *Government Executive*, May 8, 2014.

93 **the transit employee in Boston:** Richard Weir, "MBTA Worker Fired Over Assault Rap Wins Back Job," *Boston Herald*, April 14, 2011. In California, a nurse's aide who stole money from patients and a hospital employee who beat a disabled patient with a shoe could not be held accountable. Their firings were overturned by the state Personnel Board, which determined that the firings were not consistent with "progressive discipline." See Jack Dolan, "Little-Known State Board Overturns Employee Terminations," *Los Angeles Times*, November 3, 2011.

93 **"one hearing that I watched":** Steven Brill, *Tailspin* (New York: Penguin Random House, 2018), 265–66.

94 **"lack of oversight":** Brill, *Tailspin*, 262–63.

94 **2016 GAO report:** Robert Goldenkoff, "Federal Workforce: Distribution of Performance Ratings Across the Federal Government, 2013," GAO-16-520R (Washington, DC: GAO, 2016), 5. See also Joe Davidson, "Report Says 99% of Feds 'Fully Successful' or Better at Work. Is that credible?," *Washington Post*, June 14, 2016: "Feds deserve much respect, but rating more than 99 percent as fully successful strains credibility. It diminishes the truly successful and could deny the less successful the assistance they need to improve. The report gives a boost to those who seek to overhaul the civil service system, which critics say is short on employee accountability."

94 **A 2018 exposé:** Kate Taylor, "A New Principal Pushes for Change. Then the Investigations Start," *New York Times*, June 3, 2018.

95 **a theme of gray futility:** See Marshall Dimock, "Bureaucracy Self-examined," in *Reader in Bureaucracy*, ed. Robert K. Merton (New York: Macmillan, 1952), 400: "When an individual in an organization feels utterly secure, the sense of struggle which produces much

of the world's best effort is lost. Lassitude results. Laziness gradually translates itself into managerial slothfulness, one of bureaucracy's worst faults."

95 **"institutional neurosis":** Scott, *Seeing Like a State*, 349: "We have learned enough of such settings to know that over time they can produce among their inmates a characteristic institutional neurosis marked by apathy, withdrawal, lack of initiative and spontaneity, uncommunicativeness, and intractability. The neurosis is an accommodation to a deprived, bland, monotonous, controlled environment that is ultimately stupefying."

95 **An appointed official in the Pentagon:** Interview by author with former Pentagon official, 2008.

95 **A regional head of FEMA:** Charles Peters, *How Washington Really Works* (New York: Basic Books, 1992), 59.

96 **"absence of responsibility and accountability":** Report of the Expert Panel, *BH vs. Sheldon* Consent Decree, U.S. District Court for the Northern District of Illinois, July 21, 2015.

96 **"quiet crisis":** The National Commission on the Public Service, "Leadership for America: Rebuilding the Public Service" (Washington, DC: 1989), ix, 1, 3, 45.

96 **"the protections provided":** National Commission on the Public Service, "Urgent Business for America: Revitalizing the Federal Government for the 21st Century" (2003), 12.

96 **"a relic of a bygone era":** Partnership for Public Service, "Building the Enterprise: A New Civil Service Framework," April 1, 2014, 7.

97 **humans are motivated more by challenge:** See Edward Deci, *Why We Do What We Do: Understanding Self-Motivation* (New York: Penguin, 1995).

97 **he asked for volunteers:** Interview by author with Dr. James Curran, 2018.

98 **How the Worm Got in the Apple:** See Gerald E. Frug, "Does the Constitution Prevent the Discharge of Civil Service Employees?," *University of Pennsylvania Law Review* 124 (1976), and Paul P. Van Riper, *History of the United States Civil Service* (Evanston, IL: Row, Peterson, 1958). See also Philip K. Howard, "Civil Service Reform: Reassert the

President's Constitutional Authority," *The American Interest,* January 28, 2017.

98 **"system open to cronyism and subjectivity":** "Kelley: NTEU Will Continue Vocal Opposition To Administration Proposal to Remake Civil Service," press release from the National Treasury Employees Union, February 28, 2006.

98 **"the merit system":** Paul Van Riper, *History of the United States Civil Service,* 8.

98 **many of the best:** James K. Conant, "Universities and the Future of the Public Service," in *Public Service: Callings, Commitments and Contributions,* ed. Marc Holzer (2000, repr. New York: Routledge, 2018).

98 **"profound respect and admiration":** Herbert Kaufman, *The Forest Ranger: A Study in Administrative Behavior,* 2nd ed. (1960; repr. Washington, DC: RFF Press, 2006), 165.

99 **"subordinate executive officers":** *Myers v. United States,* 272 U.S. 52 (1926).

99 **"the President should possess alone the power of removal":** James Madison, *Annals of Congress,* 1st Cong., 1st sess., 518.

99 **the spoils system:** See Arthur M. Schlesinger Jr., *The Age of Jackson* (Boston: Back Bay Books, 1988), 45–46: "While helping to build the party, the spoils system also contributed to the main objective of helping restore faith in the government.... The doctrine of rotation-in-office was thus in large part conceived as a sincere measure of reform."

99 **"Tell all the office seekers to come":** Abraham Lincoln, quoted in Adam Bellow, *In Praise of Nepotism* (New York: Doubleday 2003), 356. A different version of the quote appears in David Herbert Donald, *Lincoln* (New York: Simon & Schuster, 1995), 467.

100 **"did not restrict the President's general power":** Frug, "Does the Constitution Prevent the Discharge of Civil Service Employees?," 955. See Howard, "Civil Service Reform."

100 **"seal up incompetency":** National Civil Service Reform League, "Proceedings at the Annual Meeting of The National Civil-Service Reform League," August 1, 1883, 24–25.

100 **The main constraints on firing:** See Howard, "Civil Service Reform.".

100 **"examination of witnesses, trial, or hearing":** Executive Order 101, July 27, 1897, provided protection against politically motivated firings. President Theodore Roosevelt then clarified the order: "Nothing contained in said rule shall be construed to require the examination of witnesses or any trial or hearing," Executive Order 173, May 29, 1902. These Executive Orders were codified in the Lloyd-LaFollette Act of 1912, requiring notice in writing, a chance to respond in writing, but no "examination of witnesses, trial, or hearing." See Howard, "Civil Service Reform."

100 **"illimitable power of removal":** *Humphrey's Executor v. United States,* 295 U.S. 602, 627 (1935).

100 **"The process of collective bargaining":** Franklin D. Roosevelt, "Letter on the Resolution of Federation of Federal Employees Against Strikes in Federal Service," The American Presidency Project, August 16, 1937.

101 **JFK's executive order:** Daniel DiSalvo, *Government Against Itself* (Oxford University Press, 2015), 48–50.

101 **In 1967, New York authorized collective bargaining:** DiSalvo, *Government Against Itself,* 49–50.

101 **In 1968, California followed:** DiSalvo, *Government Against Itself,* 51–52.

101 **as historian Daniel DiSalvo recounts:** "The Trouble with Public Sector Unions," *National Affairs,* Fall 2010.

101 **"We have the ability":** Victor Gotbaum, as quoted in "Captive Politicians," *New York Times,* July 9, 1975.

101 **"the severity of depriving a person":** *Cleveland Board of Education v. Loudermill,* 470 U.S. 532, 543 (1985).

102 **Civil Service Reform Act of 1978:** See Howard, "Civil Service Reform."

103 **The Partnership for Public Service proposes:** Partnership for Public Service, "Building the Enterprise: A New Civil Service Framework," April 1, 2014, 8, 30.

103 **termination review committees:** Jeffrey Liker and Michael Hoseus, *Toyota Culture* (New York: McGraw Hill, 2008), 414–18.

104 **the constitutional question:** See Howard, "Civil Service Reform."

104 **"If any power whatsoever is in its nature executive":** James Madison, "Speech in Congress on Presidential Removal Power," in James Madison, *Writings* (New York: Library of America, 1999), 456.

105 **three executive orders:** Developing Efficient, Effective, and Cost-Reducing Approaches To Federal Sector Collective Bargaining, Exec. Order No. 13836, 83 Fed. Reg. 106 (May 25, 2018); Ensuring Transparency, Accountability, and Efficiency in Taxpayer-Funded Union Time Use, Exec. Order No. 13837, 83 Fed. Reg. 106 (May 25, 2018); Promoting Accountability and Streamlining Removal Procedures Consistent With Merit System Principles, Exec. Order No. 13839, 83 Fed. Reg. 106 (May 25, 2018); see also Philip K. Howard, "Impartial Advisers Could Help Trump Restore Civil Service Accountability," *The Hill*, June 4, 2018.

106 **"Sweetening pension benefits":** Jim Dwyer, "New York Has Given Away the Keys to More Than a Prius," *New York Times*, May 15, 2018.

106 **Illinois is functionally bankrupt:** Andrew Schroedter and Patrick Rehkamp, "Six Figure Pension Payments Soar," Better Government Association, September 13, 2015.

106 **El Monte, California:** Jack Dolan, "When City Retirement Pays Better Than the Job," *Los Angeles Times*, December 30, 2016.

106 **"essential services are slashed . . . less with less":** Mary William Walsh, "A $76,000 Monthly Pension: Why States and Cities are Short on Cash," *New York Times*, April 14, 2018.

107 **"The community requires liberty":** See Reinhold Niebuhr, *Children of Light and Children of Darkness* (Chicago: University of Chicago Press, 2011), 3.

108 **"the liberated individual and the controlling state":** Patrick J. Deneen, *Why Liberalism Failed* (New Haven: Yale University Press, 2018), 38. "With the liberation of individuals from [family, church, and community], there is more need to regulate behavior through the imposition of positive law. At the same time, as the authority of social norms dissipates, they are increasingly felt to be residual, arbitrary, and oppressive, motivating calls for the state to actively work toward their eradication."

108 **"contentment within the organization":** Hayek, *Constitution of Liberty,* 122.

108 **"middle layers of society":** Levin, *Fractured Republic.*

109 **"The true test of a good government":** Alexander Hamilton, "No. 68," *The Federalist Papers* (New York: Modern Library, 2001), 438.

Chapter 9: Governing Institutions Must Govern

110 **"The infirmities most besetting":** Letter to John Cartwright, in *Selections from the Private Correspondence of James Madison: From 1813 to 1836* (Washington: JC McGuire, 1824), 53. See also John Jay, in *The Speeches of the Different Governors, to the Legislature of the State of New York* (Albany, NY: J. B. van Steenbergh, 1825), 48: "Laws and regulations, however carefully devised, frequently prove defective in practice."

111 **epidemic of defensiveness:** George Priest, "The Modern Transformation of Civil Law," Buffalo Law Review 54 (2006): 957; Walter Olson, *The Litigation Explosion: What Happened When America Unleashed the Lawsuit* (New York: Truman Talley, 1992). Philip K. Howard, *The Collapse of the Common Good* (New York: Ballantine, 2002), 3–35.

111 **264-foot fishing trawler:** Colin Grabow, "The Jones Act Drives America's Finest into Exile," *Wall Street Journal,* April 29, 2018.

112 **25 percent of total K-12 budgets:** The federal government does not collect data on national special education costs, but 25 percent is a conservative estimate based on available data and interviews with school administrators and experts. Budgets of individual school districts suggest the number is often much higher. For example, in 2005, Washington, DC, spent one-third of its budget on special education. Dan Keating and V. Dion Haynes, "Special-Ed Tuition a Growing Drain on D.C.," *Washington Post,* June 5, 2006. In a study by the Economic Policy Institute of nine school districts across the country (including only one large urban district, Los Angeles), the average district spent 21 percent of total spending on special education, with one district's expenditures at 30 percent for one year. Juan Diego Alonso and Richard Rothstein, "Where Has the Money Been Going?: A Pre-

liminary Update," Economic Policy Institute Briefing Paper #281, October 28, 2010, 5, 11. Costs have continued to grow since then. Special education costs in Massachusetts increased by 56 percent from 2006 to 2012. "The Bottom Line Report: Understanding Rising Special Education Costs in Massachusetts and The Real Cost to State Taxpayers," Massachusetts Association of 766 Approved Private Schools, December 2012. California schools have reported a 55 percent growth in special education costs from 2006 to 2016. Maya Srikrishnan, "Special Education Costs Are Rising," *New America Weekly*, February 8, 2018. The Economic Policy Institute study as well as other reports of special education costs do not include general education expenditures attributable to students with disabilities.

112 **about $150 billion a year:** Based on total expenditures for elementary and secondary education in the 2014–2015 school year: US Department of Education, National Center for Education Statistics, Revenues and Expenditures for Public Elementary and Secondary Education: School Year 2014–15 (Fiscal Year 2015) First Look, NCES 2018-301 (Washington, DC: U.S. Department of Education, 2018).

112 **farm subsidies from the New Deal:** According to the Environmental Working Group's Farm Subsidy Database, farm subsidies totaled $353.5 billion between 1995 and 2016, for an average of $16 billion a year. Environmental Working Group, "The United States Farm Subsidy Information." See also "Milking Taxpayers," *Economist*, February 12, 2015.

112 **the Davis-Bacon law:** See James Sherk, "Repealing the Davis–Bacon Act Would Save Taxpayers $10.9 Billion," Heritage Foundation, February 14, 2011; Tim Worstall, "Union Wages Increase Construction Costs By 20% - Abolish Davis Bacon," *Forbes*, August 31, 2016.

112 **The 1920 Jones Act:** See Niraj Choksi, "Trump Waives Jones Act for Puerto Rico, Easing Hurricane Shipments," *New York Times*, September 28, 2017.

112 **"the law of the land":** Author conversation with Jim Cooper, May 2018. See also Tom A. Coburn, MD, "Help Wanted: How Federal Job Training Programs Are Failing Workers," February 2011; US Government Accountability Office, "Multiple Employment and Training Programs: Providing Information on Colocating Services and Consolidating Administrative Structures Could Promote Efficiencies," GAO-

11-92 (Washington, DC: GAO, 2011); and Coburn, "What Works (and What Doesn't): The Good, the Bad, and the Ugly of Federal Job Training in Oklahoma," July 2012.

113 **David Fahrenthold:** "What Does Rural Mean? Uncle Sam Has More Than a Dozen Answers," *Washington Post*, June 8, 2013. Between December 2012 and December 2013, Fahrenthold wrote numerous articles documenting broken government programs. His 2014 "Breaking Points" series took an in-depth look at six of them. See Fahrenthold, "Sinkhole of Bureaucracy," *Washington Post*, March 22, 2014.

113 **a "small business":** Robert Jay Dilger, "Small Business Size Standards: A Historical Analysis of Contemporary Issues," R40860 (Washington, DC: Congressional Research Service, 2018), 2.

113 **"Made in USA":** Federal Trade Commission, "Complying with the Made in USA Standard."

113 **Peter Schuck's book:** Schuck, *Why Government Fails So Often* (Princeton: Princeton University Press, 2014), 190–91.

113 **Regulations from the Executive in Need of Scrutiny Act:** REINS Act, H.R. 26, 115th Cong. (2017).

113 **Germany . . . evaluates the regulatory impact of laws:** www .bundesregierung.de/Content/EN/_Anlagen/2016-08-31-2016-work-programme-on-better-regulation.pdf?__blob=publicationFile&v=1. This is a government document explaining the "Work Programme on Better Regulation."

114 **"Laws are not made for the statute books":** Angela Merkel, Welcome Letter for "Better Regulation 2016: More time for the essentials," May 2017.

114 **UK's worker safety framework:** UK worker safety laws, hse.gov.uk. For a comparison of the UK's enforcement of worker safety rules versus other European systems, see Florentin Blanc, "From Chasing Violations to Managing Risks," doctoral thesis, Universiteit Leiden, 2016, https://openaccess.leidenuniv.nl/handle/1887/44710.

114 **fifth from last:** OECD Product Market Statistics, Economy-Wide Regulation, https://www.oecd-ilibrary.org/economics/data/oecd-product -market-regulation-statistics/economy-wide-regulation_data-00593- en (2013).

114 **costs of almost $1 trillion per year:** In February 2017, I wrote an

essay for the Daily Beast outlining ten areas where the federal government could save almost $1 trillion by addressing broken and/or obsolete programs: Philip K. Howard, "How Trump Can Save Almost $1 Trillion in 10 Easy Steps," Daily Beast, February 28, 2017. That starter list:

1. Cut infrastructure red tape. A six-year delay in approving large infrastructure projects more than doubles the overall cost. Savings: A one- or two-year permitting process will save at least $100 billion annually for the foreseeable future.

2. End obsolete subsidies. Farm subsidies from the New Deal cost $20 billion. The 1930 Davis-Bacon law mandates higher wages by roughly 20% on federally funded construction, costing $11 billion per year. The 1920 Jones Act (mandating US flag ships for domestic shipping) raises the price of gasoline by 15 cents per gallon. The "carried interest" favorable tax rate for certain investment firms is an effective subsidy of, by some estimates, $20 billion per year. Savings from repeal: $70 billion.

3. Simplify Medicare/Medicaid. Require new enrollees to pick an integrated care provider (e.g., Kaiser Health Plan). The current fee-for-service model adds 15% administrative costs plus skews incentives towards more care. Savings: $125 billion in reduced administrative costs plus an estimated $20 billion in avoiding unnecessary procedures, fraud, and other waste.

4. Simplify FDA approvals. The average cost of developing a new drug can run into billions—the industry estimates the average cost at about $2.5 billion. Many of these costs are in duplicative trials for products that are known to be safe, and years of extra time before coming to market. The effect is to raise drug prices. Savings: Cutting development costs for proprietary pharmaceuticals and devices by one-quarter would save $25 billion annually.

5. Create special health courts. Studies estimate that "defensive medicine"—unnecessary tests and procedures ordered by doctors to protect against potential lawsuits—costs between $45 billion and $200 billion annually. The solution is to replace jury-by-jury decisions with an expert court (like a tax court or bankruptcy court)

that enforces standards of care consistently in written rulings. Savings: $100 billion. See Philip K. Howard, "Just Medicine," *New York Times*, April 1, 2009.

6. Cut procurement red tape. The federal government spent $500 billion in 2017 on outside vendors—purchasing tanks and planes for defense, updating computer systems, and facilities maintenance, among other things. The byzantine procedures drive away many vendors, and, in the name of saving money, raise costs by amounts impossible to calculate—although competition in space procurement has saved 50 percent. Bringing the buying process in line with best commercial practices basically requires (1) creating clear lines of authority so that responsible officials are on the spot, and (2) creating oversight committees that can review large contracts. Savings: at least $50 billion.

7. Overhaul civil service. The federal government has about 2.1 million civilian employees. They work under civil service laws that make it almost impossible to terminate anyone, discourage people from taking responsibility, and foster a "can't-do" public culture. The Partnership for Public Service has recommended a reboot. Savings/increase in effectiveness: at least 25% of total personnel costs, or $65 billion.

8. Reduce cost of unfunded mandates with a "rule of reason." Absolute mandates lead to bureaucratic excess and waste. Special education, for example, now consumes over 25% of total K-12 spending—or over $150 billion annually. The Americans with Disabilities Act is another example. A solution is to amend the statutes to permit balancing of needs and practical considerations—with officials authorized to grant waivers or approve compromises on the public record. Savings: For special ed alone, at least 25%, or $40 billion.

9. Consolidate duplicative and overlapping programs. The federal government is rife with redundant offices and initiatives. A March 2018 GAO report, for example, detailed 163 federal STEM education programs spread over 13 agencies, noting that nearly all overlapped with at least one other program. US Government Accountability Office, Science, Technology, Engineering, and Mathematics Edu-

cation: Actions Needed to Better Assess the Federal Investment, GAO-18-290 (Washington, DC: GAO, 2018), 1, 13. Consolidating programs will make them work better, as well as cut waste. Savings: Hard to estimate, but saving 5% of discretionary spending (i.e., not including transfer payments) would total $60 billion.

10. Simplify complex programs by replacing most command-and-control regulations with results-based oversight. Detailed rules, while needed in certain areas (such as pollution discharge limits), are not effective for regulating complex human activities such as workplace safety, as discussed herein. Savings: Hard to calculate, but increased effectiveness of rebooting regulation would conservatively save at least 10% of the federal regulatory burden, or roughly $200 billion.

These overhauls should enjoy broad public support: none of these changes involve "deregulation" in the sense of removing government oversight or essential public services. Some would create new jobs almost immediately—cutting infrastructure red tape, for instance, would create 1.5 million jobs within two years. The challenge is to marshal broad public demand to overcome the fierce resistance of interest groups that are feeding at the trough.

114 **unavoidable reality of scarcity:** James M. Buchanan and Richard E. Wagner, *Democracy in Deficit* (New York: Academic Press, 1977), 184: "A nation cannot survive with political institutions that do not face up squarely to the essential fact of scarcity. . . . Political institutions that do not confront this fact threaten the existence of a prosperous and free society." See Robert Heineman, *Authority and the Liberal Tradition* (New Brunswick: Transaction, 1994), 2.

114 **regulations address real needs:** Edward Rubin, "Law and Legislation in the Administrative State," *Columbia Law Review* 89, no. 3 (1989), 369–426: The regulatory state "did not arise out of some lapse of moral vigilance."

114 **"more is different":** Philip Warren Anderson, quoted in Nassim Taleb, *Antifragile: Things That Gain from Disorder* (New York: Random House, 2012), 276.

115 **Different agencies operate in different silos:** There are about sixty

main federal regulatory bodies. See Clyde Wayne Crews Jr., "How Many Federal Agencies Exist? We Can't Drain The Swamp Until We Know," Forbes.com, July 5, 2017; see also Crews, "Nobody Knows How Many Federal Agencies Exist," Competitive Enterprise Institute, August 26, 2015.

115 **"people looking at a computer":** Steve Eder, "When Picking Apples on a Farm With 5,000 Rules, Watch Out for the Ladders," *New York Times*, December 27, 2017. Interviews by Matt Brown with Peter Ten Eyck in February and July 2018.

116 **Raising the roadway of the Bayonne Bridge:** Sam Roberts, "High Above the Water, but Awash in Red Tape," *New York Times*, January 2, 2014; see also Philip K. Howard, *The Rule of Nobody* (New York: W. W. Norton, 2014), 7–12.

116 **Opening a restaurant in New York:** See, e.g, Diane Cardwell, "A New Team Helps Steer Restaurateurs through a Thicket of Red Tape," *New York Times*, December 28, 2010.

116 **placement for a foster child:** Author conversation with Lise Spacapan of the state Department of Children and Family Services, 2016.

116 **forty-ninth in World Bank rankings:** World Bank Group, "Doing Business 2018: Reforming to Create Jobs," 202.

117 **"whole-of-government" approach:** See OECD, "Recommendation of the Council on Regulatory Policy and Governance," 2012: governments should "ensure that regulation serves whole-of-government policy."

117 **"one-stop shops":** Discussions with OECD officials Nikolai Malyshev and Daniel Trnka, March 2018. See generally PricewaterhouseCoopers, "Transforming the Citizen Experience: One Stop Shop for Public Services," April 2016; World Bank Group, "Doing Business 2018: Reforming to Create Jobs," 15th ed.

117 **a 311 line:** See Steven Johnson, "What a Hundred Million Calls to 311 Reveal About New York," *Wired*, November 1, 2010. Pricewaterhouse-Coopers, "Transforming the Citizen Experience," 10.

117 **draw on best practices from other countries:** Author conversation with Nikolai Malyshev, OECD, June 2018, and OECD (2014), Regulatory Enforcement and Inspections, OECD Best Practice Principles for Regulatory Policy, OECD Publishing, 27–31.

117 **"direct regulators' efforts":** National Audit Office (UK), "Regu-

latory Quality: How Regulators Are Implementing the Hampton Vision" (2008), 10.

118 **collaborative approach to regulation:** OECD Best Practices (2014); see Blanc, "From Chasing Violations to Managing Risks."

118 **best way to create simplified codes:** For recodifications through history, see:

1. Justinian Code: D. J. Osler, "Budaeus and Roman Law," Ius Commune 13 (1985), http://data.rg.mpg.de/iuscommune/ic13_osler .pdf; *Justinian's Institutes,* trans. Peter Birks and Grant McLeod (Ithaca, NY: Cornell University Press, 1987), 11.

2. Napoleonic Code: James R. Maxeiner, "Costs of No Codes," *Mississippi College Law Review* 31 (2013): 363, 379–80; H. A. L. Fisher, "The Codes," in *Cambridge Modern History* (New York: Macmillan, 1906), 9: 151; Jean Louis Bergel, "Principal Features and Methods of Codification," *Louisiana Law Review* 48, (1988): 1073. Napoleon considered the new code his greatest accomplishment. See Bergel, supra at 1078–79: "While in exile in Saint Helena, Napoleon said, 'My true glory is not that I have won forty battles. Waterloo will blow away the memory of these victories. What nothing can blow away, what will live eternally is my Civil Code.'"

3. German codes: See, for example, Konrad Zweigert and Hein Kötz, *An Introduction to Comparative Law,* 3rd ed., trans. Tony Weir (Oxford: Clarendon, 1998), 98; and Xavier Blanc-Jouvan, "Worldwide Influence of the French Civil Code, on the Occasion of Its Bicentennial Celebration," Cornell Law School Berger International Speaker Papers 3, September 27, 2004, http://scholarship .law.cornell.edu/biss_papers/3.

4. Uniform Commercial Code: See Lawrence M. Friedman, "Business Law in an Age of Change," in *American Law in the 20th Century* (New Haven: Yale University Press, 2002), 377–98.

119 **"base closing commissions":** Jerry Brito, "Running for Cover: The BRAC Commission as a Model for Federal Spending," *Georgetown Journal of Law and Public Policy* 9 (2011), 131. See Kenneth R. Mayer, The Base Realignment and Closure Process: Is it possible to make

rational policy?" (NYU Wagner, 2007). See also George Schlossberg, "How Congress Cleared the Bases: A Legislative History of BRAC," *Journal of Defense Communities* 1 (2012).

119 **Simpson-Bowles Commission:** The commission held its first meeting on April 27, 2010 (Jackie Calmes, "Obama Tells Debt Commission 'Everything Has to Be on the Table,'" *New York Times*, April 27, 2010). It voted on its proposal on December 3, 2010 (Jeanne Sahadi, "Debt Plan Draws Bipartisan Support," CNN, December 3, 2010).

119 **"Dress appropriately":** Leah Fessler, "GM's Dress Code Is Only Two Words," Quartz, April 3, 2018. Soon after implementing the policy, Barra received pushback from a senior manager who worried that members of his team, who on occasion had to meet with government officials, wouldn't be presentable. She encouraged him to talk to the team. He soon called back to say that they had settled on a plan—the four people in question would keep a pair of dress pants at work. Barra describes this as "a big 'a-ha' moment" for herself and the company: "'What I realized is that you really need to make sure your managers are empowered—because if they cannot handle "dress appropriately," what other decisions can they handle? And I realized that often, if you have a lot of overly prescriptive policies and procedures, people will live down to them. . . . But if you let people own policies themselves— especially at the first level of people supervision—it helps develop them. It was an eye-opening experience, but I now know that these small little things changed our culture powerfully. They weren't the only factor, but they contributed significantly.'"

120 **Congress has a 12 percent confidence rating:** Frank Newport, "Americans' Confidence in Institutions Edges Up," Gallup, June 26, 2017.

120 **critics Thomas Mann and Norman Ornstein explain:** See Mann and Ornstein, *The Broken Branch* (Oxford: Oxford University Press, 2008), 6–11; Mann and Ornstein, *It's Even Worse Than It Looks* (New York: Basic Books, 2016), xix–xxi, 3–8, 17–18.

121 **They particularly blame Republicans:** Mann and Ornstein, *It's Even Worse than It Looks*, xi–xvii, 42–43, 51–58, 101–10, 184–87; Mann and Ornstein, "How the Republicans Broke Congress," *New York Times*, December 2, 2017.

121 **Most of the important decisions:** See Lyndon B. Johnson School of Public Affairs, "The Reclamation of the U.S. Congress," 2013, 9–13, 69–70; Kevin Kosar and Adam Chan, "A Case for Stronger Congressional Committees," R Street, August 2016.

121 **comedian George Carlin:** C-SPAN 2, Washington, DC, May 19, 1999.

121 **one hundred separate committees and subcommittees:** Author conversation with Secretary Jeh Johnson, April 2015. See also "Who Oversees Homeland Security? Um, Who Doesn't?," *All Things Considered*, National Public Radio, July 20, 2010.

121 **Executive branch officials don't take Congress seriously:** Philip DeVoe, "Congressional Hearings Need Aggressive Reform," *National Review*, May 5, 2018. See Chris Swecker, "Republicans Walked Right into Peter Strzok's Trap," Fox News, July 13, 2018; Aaron Blake, "7 Key Moments from Peter Strzok's Wild Hearing," *Washington Post*, July 12, 2018.

121 **Republicans have introduced over sixty bills:** See, e.g., Chris Riotta, "GOP Aims to Kill Obamacare Yet Again After Failing 70 Times," *Time*, July 29, 2017.

122 **"takes about 95 employees":** David Fahrenthold, "Unrequired Reading: Many of the Thousands of Reports Mandated by Congress Will Only Gather Dust," *Washington Post*, May 3, 2014; Fahrenthold, "Congress Tries to Cut Down on Un-Needed Reports," *Washington Post*, May 3, 2014.

122 **shift authority back to committees:** See Bipartisan Policy Center Commission on Political Reform, "Governing in a Polarized America: A Bipartisan Blueprint to Strengthen Our Democracy," June 24, 2014, 56–69; Lyndon B. Johnson School of Public Affairs, "The Reclamation of the U.S. Congress," 39–57, 71–73; Kosar and Chan, "A Case for Stronger Congressional Committees," R Street, 2016. See generally Jason Grumet, *City of Rivals* (Guilford CT: Lyons Press, 2014).

122 **"a return to functioning committees":** Author conversation with Jim Cooper, May 2018.

122 **constitutional amendment for sunsetting laws:** See Howard, *Rule of Nobody*, 179–80. My proposed text reads: "No statute or regulation requiring expenditure of public or private resources (other than to oversee legal compliance or enforcement), shall be in force for longer

than fifteen years. Congress may reenact such a law only after finding that it continues to serve the public interest and does not unnec-
essarily conflict or interfere with other priorities. Before making its
determinations, Congress shall consider recommendations by an
independent commission on whether and how to amend any such statute or program."

122 **The Framers made a mistake:** See Howard, *Rule of Nobody*, 136–37.

123 **Americans overwhelmingly distrust justice:** Regina Corso and
Elizabeth Shores, "Public Trust of Civil Justice," HarrisInteractive,
June 20, 2005, 6.

123 **culture of defensiveness:** Priest, "The Modern Transformation of
Civil Law"; Olson, *Litigation Explosion*; Philip K. Howard, *The Collapse of the Common Good* (New York: Ballantine, 2002).

124 **hovering over children . . . stunts their emotional growth:** See,
e.g., Hanna Rosin, "The Overprotected Kid," *Atlantic*, April 2014;
Ellen Barry March, "In Britain's Playgrounds, 'Bringing in Risk' to
Build Resilience," *New York Times*, March 10, 2018; Andrea Petersen,
"The Overprotected American Child," *Wall Street Journal*, June
1, 2018; Lenore Skenazy, *Free-Range Kids, How to Raise Safe, Self-
Reliant Children (Without Going Nuts with Worry)* (San Francisco:
Jossey-Bass, 2010); Richard Louv, *Last Child in the Woods: Saving Our
Children From Nature-Deficit Disorder* (Chapel Hill, NC: Algonquin
Books, 2008); Hara Estroff Marano, *A Nation of Wimps: The High Cost
of Invasive Parenting* (New York: Crown Archetype, 2008); Tim Gill,
No Fear: Growing Up in a Risk-Averse Society (London: Calouste Gul-
benkian Foundation, 2007); Philip K. Howard, *Life Without Lawyers*
(New York: W. W. Norton, 2009), 34–48.

124 **"defensive medicine" costs society $45–200 billion:** $45 billion:
Michelle M. Mello, et al., "National Costs of the Medical Liability Sys-
tem," *Health Affairs* 29, no. 9 (September 2010): 1574; $200 billion:
PricewaterhouseCoopers' Health Research Institute, "The Price of
Excess: Identifying Waste in Healthcare Spending," 2008, 1.

124 **"Choosing among values":** Charles Wyzanski, "Equal Justice
through Law," 47 *Tulane Law Review*, no. 4 (1973): 951, 959.

125 **"Who am I to judge":** Author conversation with Judge Robert
Scott, 1995.

125 **sue his drycleaners:** See Jim Avila, et al., "Judge Rules in Favor of Dry Cleaners in $54 Million Pants Lawsuit," ABC News, June 25, 2007; Howard, *Rule of Nobody,* 54.

125 **"act is illegal":** Donald J. Black, "The Mobilization of Law," *Journal of Legal Studies* 2 (1973): 131 n. 24.

126 **what people can sue for:** For example of a sledding verdict, see Patrick Healy, "Town's Downhill Pastime May Face an Uphill Fight," *New York Times,* April 26, 2004; Karen Sloan, "Lawsuit Fears Close Two Omaha Sled Slopes," *Omaha World-Herald,* January 3, 2007, http://archives.starbulletin.com/2006/07/26/news/story03.html;   Carol Stark, "Fun May Be Next on the Banned List," *Joplin* [MO] *Globe,* December 7, 2007; and, in a happy reversal, Edward Sieger, "Update: Easton, PA Overturns Sledding Ban," [Pennsylvania] *ExpressTimes,* December 13, 2007. In 2006, the American Bar Association declined to sponsor a surfing event, for fear that one of its members might get hurt and sue. See Stewart Yerton, "Liabilities scare lawyers' group away from surf meet," *Honolulu Star Bulletin,* July 26, 2006.

126 **Lord Hoffmann held:** *Tomlinson v. Congleton Borough Council* [2003] UKHL 47 . See discussion in Philip K. Howard, *Life Without Lawyers* (New York: W. W. Norton, 2009), 15–16.

126 **"dependent upon the whim of the particular jury":** Oliver Wendell Holmes Jr., "Law in Science and Science in Law," *Harvard Law Review* 12 (1899): 443, 458.

127 **a coercive use of state power:** See discussion in Howard, *Collapse of the Common Good,* 40–56.

127 **Some prominent scholars and judges agree with me:** See *Munn v. Hotchkiss School,* US Court of Appeals No. 14-2410 (2nd Cir. 2015): "To impose a duty on Connecticut schools to warn about or protect against risks as remote as tick-borne encephalitis might discourage field trips that serve important educational roles. See generally Howard, *Collapse of the Common Good.* If the costs imposed on schools and nonprofit organizations become too high, such trips might be curtailed or cease completely, depriving children of valuable opportunities. Public policy may thus require that participants bear the risks of unlikely injuries and illnesses such as the one that occurred in this case so that institutions can continue to offer these activities."

See discussion in William H. Simon, "Solving Problems vs. Claiming Rights," *William and Mary Law Review* 46, no. 1 (2004): 149, 151: "The American tort system has radical deficiencies that one would expect liberals to decry. The system provides no benefits at all to most injured people.... The awards the system does make are staggeringly arbitrary, depending on the actual or anticipated judgments ... of panels of lay decisionmakers ... operating under vague instructions and without any knowledge of decisions in other cases.... The system's effect in deterring bad conduct seems weak, and in some respects, perverse.... Less than fifty percent of the total payments by defendants go to claimants, and in some categories, much less.... 'Close to two-thirds of insurance company expenditures in asbestos suits (including cases settled before trial) ended up in the pockets of lawyers and experts for both sides rather than in those of asbestos victims and their families.'"

127 **vital public choices that no one today is making:** Diplomat George Kennan recommended creating a powerless fourth branch of government, a "Council of State" whose only job was to comment on how the other branches were doing. A credible outside voice could cut through the partisan cacophony and point fingers at officials and institutions that are falling down on the job. See George F. Kennan, *Around the Cragged Hill: A Personal and Political Philosophy* (New York: W. W. Norton, 1993), 232–49. I don't think that the oversight council needs to be official; it just needs to have moral authority and enough financial support to produce the reports and events needed to expose the abject failures of Congress and the executive branch to fulfill their responsibilities. Equally important, it must not be located in Washington, or it will soon be worn down by the culture.

128 **"But we, we have no sense":** Edna St. Vincent Millay, "We have gone too far." Millay, *Collected Poems* (New York: Harper 1956), 427; reprinted in *Lapham's Quarterly* 10, no. 2 (Spring 2016).

Chapter 10: Revive the Moral Mandate

130 **"There are no great men":** Alexis de Tocqueville, *Democracy in America*, ed. Phillips Bradley, 2 vols. (New York: Vintage, 1990), 1: 244.

130 **"Epochs sometimes occur":** Tocqueville, *Democracy in America*, 1: 242–43.

131 **We need to figure this out anew:** See Václav Havel, *The Art of the Impossible: Politics as Morality in Practice* (New York: Knopf, 1997), 121: We need to "come to a new understanding of ourselves, our limitations, and our place in the world." See also Friedrich A. Hayek, *The Road to Serfdom* (Chicago: University of Chicago Press, 2007), 65. "We are ready to accept almost any explanation of the present crisis of our civilization," Hayek suggested, "except one . . . that the present state of the world may be the result of genuine error on our own part, and that the pursuit of some of our most cherished ideals has apparently produced results utterly different from those . . . we expected."

132 **We no longer believe in belief:** See Mary Ann Glendon, *Rights Talk: The Impoverishment of Political Discourse* (New York: Free Press, 1991), 14: "Lacking a grammar of cooperative living, we are like a traveler who can say a few words to get a meal and a room in a foreign city, but cannot converse with its inhabitants." See Michael Polanyi, *Personal Knowledge* (Chicago: University of Chicago Press, 1962), 228. "The modern mind, tortured by moral self-doubt," Polanyi said, "indulge[s] its moral passions" with "ruthless objectivity."

132 **they will not "make the rules":** At his confirmation hearing, Chief Justice Roberts reiterated the required incantation that judges "don't make the rules; they apply them."

132 **making that "value judgment":** Author conversation with Professor Jonathan Friedman, March 2018.

132 **causes our virtues to degenerate:** Michael Sandel, *Democracy's Discontent: America in Search of a Public Philosophy* (Cambridge, MA: Belknap Press, 1998), 6, 322: The procedural republic "cannot secure the liberty it promises because it cannot inspire the sense of community and civic engagement that liberty requires."

132 **"because he lives in society":** Emile Durkheim, "Division of Labor in Society: Conclusion," in *Emile Durkheim on Morality and Society*, ed. Robert N. Bellah (Chicago: University of Chicago Press, 1973), 137.

133 **"social capital":** See generally Francis Fukuyama, "Social Capital," in Lawrence E. Harrison and Samuel P. Huntington, eds., *Culture*

Matters: How Values Shape Human Progress (New York: Basic, 2000); Robert Putnam, *Bowling Alone: The Collapse and Revival of American Community* (New York: Simon & Schuster, 2001).

133 **Between 'can do' and 'may do':** John Fletcher Moulton, "Law and Manners," *Atlantic*, July 1924.

133 **"Only a virtuous people":** Benjamin Franklin, Letter to the Abbés Chalut and Arnoux, April 1, 1787. www.franklinpapers.org/franklin/framedVolumes.jsp?vol=44&page=605

133 **"No government can continue good":** Thomas Jefferson, Letter to John Adams, December 10, 1819, http://rotunda.upress.virginia.edu/founders/default.xqy?keys=FOEA-print-04-02-02-0953.

133 **Americans no longer share the same values:** But see Alan Wolfe, *One Nation, After All* (New York: Penguin, 1999), who found that Americans are not fractured on the foundational values needed for a healthy society.

134 **"Men are qualified for civil":** Edmund Burke, quoted in Robert Nisbet, *Twilight of Authority* (Carmel, IN: Liberty Fund, 2000), 64.

134 **Distrust breeds fear:** Leszek Kolakowski, *Modernity on Endless Trial* (Chicago: University of Chicago Press, 1990), 162–74, referring to the "self-poisoning of the open society." See also Michael Lerner, *Surplus Powerlessness: The Psychodynamics of Everyday Life* (1979; repr. Oakland: Institute for Labor and Mental Health, 1986), 210: "Ethical relativism is a powerful tool for disempowering people."

135 **"A brackish tide of pessimism":** David Brooks, "The Age of Skepticism," *New York Times*, December 1, 2005.

135 **"You have no right":** Frederick Douglass, "What to the Slave is the Fourth of July?," *The Portable Frederick Douglass* (New York: Penguin Classics, 2016), 203. Historian Niall Ferguson concludes that "the biggest challenge facing mature democracies is how to restore the social contract between the generations"; Ferguson, *The Great Degeneration: How Institutions Decay and Economies Die* (New York: Penguin, 2013), 43–44.

135 **"lacks moral resonance":** Sandel, *Democracy's Discontent*, 322.

136 **"to refrain from belief":** Polanyi, *Personal Knowledge*, 271.

136 **"Fundamentalists rush in":** Sandel, *Democracy's Discontent*, 322.

137 **"anti-culture":** Patrick J. Deneen, *Why Liberalism Failed* (New Haven: Yale University Press, 2018), 64–91.

137 **"The result of a consistent . . . substitution":** Hannah Arendt, "Truth and Politics," in *The Portable Hannah Arendt* (New York: Penguin Classics 2003), 568.

137 **"To act morally is to do good":** Emile Durkheim, *Selected Writings*, ed. Anthony Giddens (Cambridge: Cambridge University Press, 1972), 110.

137 **good values are manifested in actions:** see Aristotle, *Nicomachean Ethics* (Oxford: Oxford University Press, 2009), 28: "It is well said, then, that it is by doing just acts that the just man is produced."

137 **cannot be prescribed in advance:** See Durkheim, *Selected Writings*, 112: "Circumstances are never the same, and as a consequence the rules of morality must be applied intelligently."

137 **It all boils down:** Aristotle, *Nicomachean Ethics*, 112.

138 **pulling up a plant:** Onora O'Neill, "A Question of Trust," The BBC Reith Lectures 2002 (Cambridge: University of Cambridge Press, 2002), 19.

138 **"All acts are so tied together":** John Dewey, *Theory of the Moral Life* (New York: Irvington Publishers, 1996), 12. See also Ralph Waldo Emerson, "The Over-Soul," *Essays and Lectures* (New York: Library of America, 1983), 386: The moral man "speaks from his character and not from his tongue." Leslie Stephen, the father of Virginia Woolf, made the point that morality is embedded within a person, not in this or that act: "Morality is internal. The moral law . . . has to be expressed in the form 'Be this,' not in the form 'Do this.'" Leslie Stephen, *The Science of Ethics* (Cambridge: Cambridge University Press 2011), 155.

138 **Dewey considered evaluations of character:** Dewey, *Theory of the Moral Life*, 20: "For practical reasons we must be concerned with character in our daily affairs. Whether we buy or sell goods, lend money or invest in securities, call a physician or consult a lawyer, take or refuse advice from a friend, fall in love and marry, the ultimate outcome depends upon the characters which are involved."

139 **"The freedom of the subjective person":** Polanyi, *Personal Knowledge*, 309.

139 **leadership might as well be illegal:** See Warren Bennis, *Why Leaders Can't Lead* (San Francisco: Jossey-Bass, 1989), xiii, observing an "unconscious conspiracy that prevents leaders from taking charge."

139 **"We are still incapable of understanding":** Václav Havel, Address to Congress, February 22, 1990; Havel, *The Art of the Impossible: Politics as Morality in Practice* (New York: Knopf, 1997), 19.

140 **"It would seem as if the rulers":** Tocqueville, *Democracy in America*, 2: 329.

140 **"social norms and rules which are accompanied":** Emile Durkheim, *Ethics and the Sociology of Morals*, introduction by Robert Hall (New York: Prometheus Books, 1993), 19. See Durkheim, *Selected Writings*, 113: "Thus, it does not follow from a belief in the need for discipline that it must be blind and slavish. Moral rules must be invested with the authority without which they would be ineffective."

141 **"We are determined to respect everyone":** Christopher Lasch, *The Revolt of the Elites* (New York: W. W. Norton, 1996), 89, 107.

141 **to revive shaming:** Robert Reich, *The Common Good* (New York: Knopf, 2018), 131–55.

141 **The book to read:** Greg Lukianoff and Jonathan Haidt, *The Coddling of the American Mind* (New York: Penguin, 2018).

142 **"They develop an interest":** Francis Fukuyama, "Social Capital," in Harrison and Huntington, eds., *Culture Matters*, 108: "If people know that they have to continue to live with one another in bounded communities in which continued cooperation will be rewarded, they develop an interest in their own reputations, as well as in the monitoring and punishment of those who violate community rules."

142 **"Democracy does not give people":** Tocqueville, *Democracy in America*, 1: 252.

142 **"is fit only to enervate":** Tocqueville, *Democracy in America*, 1: 87. See also Tom Friedman, *Thank You for Being Late* (New York: Picador 2017), 355: "Wherever possible, the thrust of federal government should shift from offering solutions driven by the national bureau-

cracy to incentivizing, enabling, and inspiring experimentation and innovation from the local and individual level upward."

142 **a doctrine called "subsidiarity":** Pope John Paul II, Centesimus Annus: Encyclical Letter on the Hundredth Anniversary of *Rerum Novarum*, May 1, 1991: "A community of a higher order should not interfere in the internal life of a community of a lower order, depriving the latter of its functions, but rather should support it in case of need and help to coordinate its activity with the activities of the rest of society, always with a view to the common good." See also Samuel Fleischacker, *A Third Concept of Liberty* (Princeton: Princeton University Press, 1999), 131. See generally Amitai Etzioni, *The New Golden Rule* (New York: Basic Books, 1996).

142 **take more responsibility for social services:** See Robert Bellah et al., *The Good Society* (New York: Vintage Books, 1992), 262, giving the example of "a summer program for teenagers sponsored by a black church in a depressed neighborhood." More authority at the local level opens the door to a wide range of tailored solutions that not only better address the issue, but also engage the community. See also Charles F. Sabel and William H. Simon, "Minimalism and Experimentalism in the Administrative State," *Georgetown Law Journal* 100, no. 1 (2011): 90: "Tailoring also requires an understanding of local context. A child welfare worker putting together a plan for an obese child may be able to include a bicycle in the plan if she knows that the family's church can be persuaded to come up with one if credibly assured that it will fill an important need. Police dealing with a high-crime neighborhood can be more effective if they learn from local residents that a poorly maintained house from which drugs are sold is a magnet for nonresident deviants."

143 **reduce chronic homelessness:** Interview by author of Roseanne Haggerty, July 2018; David Bornstein, "A Growing Drive to Get Homelessness to Zero," *New York Times*, June 5, 2018.

143 **Lancaster, Pennsylvania:** Tom Friedman, "Where American Politics Can Still Work: From the Bottom Up," *New York Times*, July 3, 2018.

144 **start moving agencies out of Washington:** See Philip K. Howard, "We Can't Change Washington—So Let's Dismantle It and Spread It

Around," *Daily Beast*, October 16, 2016. See also Paul Kupiec, "How the Feds can Really Spread the Wealth Around," *Wall Street Journal*, December 8, 2016; Matthew Yglesias, "Let's relocate a bunch of government agencies to the Midwest," Vox, December 9, 2016; Ross Douthat, "Break Up the Liberal City," *New York Times*, March 25, 2017; and Betsy McCaughey, "To Deregulate America, Send D.C. Bureaucrats to the Heartland," *Investor's Business Daily*, December 20, 2017.

144 **"WEBEHWYGs":** Mark A. Abramson and Paul R. Lawrence, eds., *Learning the Ropes: Insights for Political Appointees* (Lanham, MD: Rowman & Littlefield Publishers, 2005), 47.

145 **[cost of] moving agencies out of Washington:** The cost of replacing 75 percent of federal offices in Washington is on the order of $30 billion, or 1 percent of the federal budget excluding social security. The calculation is as follows: (1) Replace 74 million square feet. (Total office space owned or leased by the federal government in Washington is 96 million square feet, of which 85 percent is office and 15 percent is warehouse.) (2) Assume $300 per foot average purchase price plus $100 per foot fitting out/moving costs = $400 per foot for total moving costs. (3) Total cost to move 75 percent of agencies = $29.6 billion.

Chapter 11: Profile of a Practical Society

146 **"The ideal of true freedom":** Thomas Hill Green, *Liberal Legislation and Freedom of Contract* (Oxford: Slatery & Rose, 1861), 9.

149 **doctors waste up to half their time on paperwork:** See, e.g., Danielle Ofri, "The Patients vs. Paperwork Problem for Doctors," *New York Times*, November 14, 2017.

149 **$45–$200 billion in unnecessary "defensive medicine":** $45 billion: Michelle M. Mello, et al., "National Costs of the Medical Liability System," *Health Affairs* 29, no. 9 (September 2010): 1574; $200 billion: PricewaterhouseCoopers' Health Research Institute, "The Price of Excess: Identifying Waste in Healthcare Spending," 2008, 1.

149 **Children in other countries:** See, e.g., Ellen Barry March, "In Brit-

ain's Playgrounds, 'Bringing in Risk' to Build Resilience," *New York Times*, March 10, 2018; Tim Gill, *No Fear: Growing Up in a Risk-Averse Society* (London: Calouste Gulbenkian Foundation, 2007).

151 **"This habit of surveillance":** See Alexis de Tocqueville, *The Old Regime and the French Revolution*, trans. Stuart Gilbert (New York: Doubleday, 1983), 61–62, 69. Thanks to Lewis Lapham for pointing me to this.

Chapter 12: Who Has Responsibility for Change?

154 **"Human greatness . . . exists":** Michael Polanyi, *Personal Knowledge* (Chicago: University of Chicago Press, 1962), 380: "For human greatness . . . belongs to the family of things which exist only for those committed to them. All manner of excellence that we accept for our guidance, and all obligations to which we grant jurisdiction over us, can be defined by our respect for human greatness."

155 **the disintegration of democracy into dictatorship:** Polybius, *The Histories*, eds. Robin Waterfield and B. C. McGing (Oxford: Oxford University Press, 2010), 376, 378.

155 **"a network of small complicated rules":** Alexis de Tocqueville, *Democracy in America*, edited by Phillips Bradley, 2 vols. (New York: Vintage, 1990), 2: 319.

156 **"as an unalterable fact":** Václav Havel, "New Year's Address to the Nation, 1990," *Art of the Impossible*, 4.

157 **"a conception of purpose":** Aldous Huxley, *Brave New World* (New York: Harper Perennial, 2006), 177.

158 **"There is an amazing strength":** Tocqueville, *Democracy in America*, 1: 247: "There is an amazing strength in the expression of the will of a whole people; and when it declares itself, even the imagination of those who would wish to contest it is overawed."

Appendix: Ten Principles for a Practical Society

161 **the right thing to do in a particular situation:** See Nicola Lacey, "Jurisprudence of Discretion," in *The Uses of Discretion*, ed. Keith Hawkins, Oxford Socio-Legal Studies (Oxford: Clarendon, 1992),

380. See also M. P. Baumgartner, "The Myth of Discretion," in Hawkins, ed., *Uses of Discretion*, 129: Leaving aside a few hot-button issues, American judges of different ideological bent generally rule in ways that are "remarkably patterned and consistent."

163 **Lloyd-Lafollette Act:** See Philip K. Howard, "Civil Service Reform: Reassert the President's Constitutional Authority," *The American Interest,* January 28, 2017.

166 **Special education . . . is notoriously bureaucratic:** Miriam Kurtzig Freedman, "Special Education: Its Ethical Dilemmas, Entitlement Status, and Suggested Systemic Reforms," *University of Chicago Law Review* 79, no. 1 (2012). See also President's Commission on Excellence in Special Education, Office of Special Education and Rehabilitative Services, A New Era: Revitalizing Special Education for Children and Their Families (US Department of Education, 2002).

SELECTED BIBLIOGRAPHY

Arendt, Hannah. *The Human Condition*. Chicago: University of Chicago Press, 1958.

———. *The Portable Hannah Arendt*. New York: Penguin Classics, 2003.

Aristotle. *Nicomachean Ethics*. Oxford: Oxford University Press, 2009.

Arum, Richard. *Judging School Discipline: The Crisis of Moral Authority*. Cambridge, MA: Harvard University Press, 2003.

Ayres, Ian, and John Braithwaite. *Responsive Regulation: Transcending the Deregulation Debate*. New York: Oxford University Press, 1992.

Banfield, Edward. *The Moral Basis of a Backward Society*. New York: Free Press, 1958.

Barak, Aharon. *Judicial Discretion*. Translated by Yadin Kaufmann. New Haven: Yale University Press, 1989.

Bardach, Eugene, and Robert A. Kagan. *Going by the Book: The Problem of Regulatory Unreasonableness*. Philadelphia: Temple University Press, 1982.

Barnard, Chester Irving. *The Functions of the Executive*. Cambridge, MA: Harvard University Press, 1968.

Barzun, Jacques. *From Dawn to Decadence: 500 Years of Western Cultural Life; 1500 to the Present*. New York: HarperCollins, 2000.

———. *A Stroll with William James*. Chicago: University of Chicago Press, 2002.

Baumgartner, Frank R., and Bryan D. Jones. *Agendas and Instability in American Politics*. 2nd ed. Chicago: University of Chicago Press, 2009.

Bellah, Robert N., Richard Madsen, William M. Sullivan, Ann Swidler, and Steven M. Tipton. *The Good Society*. New York: Vintage, 1991.

Bennis, Warren G. *Why Leaders Can't Lead*. San Francisco: Jossey-Bass, 1989.

Berlin, Isaiah. *Four Essays on Liberty*. Oxford: Oxford University Press, 1969.

———. *The Proper Study of Mankind: An Anthology of Essays*. Edited by Henry Hardy and Roger Hausheer. New York: Farrar, Straus and Giroux, 2000.

Bovens, Mark. *Quest for Responsibility: Accountability and Citizenship in Complex Organizations*. Cambridge: Cambridge University Press, 1998.

Braithwaite, John, Toni Makkai, and Valerie A. Braithwaite. *Regulating Aged Care: Ritualism and the New Pyramid*. Cheltenham, UK: Edward Elgar, 2007.

Brill, Steven. *Tailspin*. New York: Penguin Random House, 2018.

Calabresi, Guido. *A Common Law for the Age of Statutes*. Cambridge, MA: Harvard University Press, 1985.

Cardozo, Benjamin N. *The Growth of the Law*. New Haven: Yale University Press, 1924.

———. *The Nature of the Judicial Process*. New Haven: Yale University Press, 1921.

Coser, Lewis. *The Functions of Social Conflict*. New York: Free Press, 1964.

Crozier, Michel. *The Bureaucratic Phenomenon*. Chicago: University of Chicago Press, 1964.

Crozier, Michel, Samuel P. Huntington, and Joōji Watanuki. *The Crisis of Democracy: Report on the Governability of Democracies to the Trilateral Commission* (New York: New York University Press, 1975).

Damasio, Antonio. *Descartes' Error*. New York: Penguin, 1994.

Deci, Edward. *Why We Do What We Do: Understanding Self-Motivation*. New York: Penguin, 1995.

Deneen, Patrick. *Why Liberalism Failed*. New Haven: Yale University Press, 2018.

Dewey, John. *Theory of the Moral Life*. New York: Irvington Publishers, 1996.

DiSalvo, Daniel. *Government Against Itself*. Oxford: Oxford University Press, 2015.

Drucker, Peter F. *The Age of Discontinuity: Guidelines to Our Changing Society*. 2nd ed. New Brunswick, NJ: Transaction, 1992.

———. *The End of Economic Man: A Study of the New Totalitarianism.* Rev. ed. Piscataway, NJ: Transaction, 1995.

———. *A Functioning Society.* New Brunswick, NJ: Transaction, 2003.

Drucker, Peter F., William V. D'Antonio, and Howard J. Ehrlich, eds. *Power and Democracy in America.* Notre Dame, IN: University of Notre Dame Press, 1961.

Durkheim, Emile. *Selected Writings.* Edited by Anthony Giddens. Cambridge: Cambridge University Press, 1972.

———. *Emile Durkheim on Morality and Society.* Edited by Robert N. Bellah. Chicago: University of Chicago Press, 1973.

Dworkin, Ronald M. *Taking Rights Seriously.* Cambridge, MA: Harvard University Press, 1978.

Eizenstat, Stuart E. *President Carter: The White House Years.* New York: St. Martin's Press, 2018.

Endicott, Timothy A. O. "The Impossibility of the Rule of Law." *Oxford Journal of Legal Studies* 19, no. 1 (Spring 1999).

Etzioni, Amitai. *The New Golden Rule.* New York: Basic Books, 1996.

Ferguson, Niall. *The Great Degeneration: How Institutions Decay and Economies Die.* New York: Penguin, 2013.

Fleischacker, Samuel. *A Third Concept of Liberty: Judgment and Freedom in Kant and Adam Smith.* Princeton: Princeton University Press, 1999.

Foner, Eric. *The Story of American Freedom.* New York: W. W. Norton, 1998.

Friedman, Tom. *Thank You for Being Late.* New York: Picador, 2017.

Fromm, Erich. *Escape from Freedom.* New York: Henry Holt, 1994.

Frug, Gerald E. "Does the Constitution Prevent the Discharge of Civil Service Employees?" *University of Pennsylvania Law Review* 124 (1976).

Furedi, Frank. *The Culture of Fear Revisited.* London: Continuum, 2006.

Fukuyama, Francis. *Political Order and Political Decay.* New York: Farrar, Straus and Giroux, 2015.

Fuller, Lon. *The Morality of Law.* New Haven: Yale University Press, 1969.

Gill, Tim. *No Fear: Growing Up in a Risk-Averse Society.* London: Calouste Gulbenkian Foundation, 2007.

Gilmore, Grant. *The Ages of American Law.* Introduction and final chapter by Philip Bobbitt. New Haven: Yale University Press, 2014.

Gladwell, Malcolm. *Blink: The Power of Thinking without Thinking.* Boston: Back Bay Books, 2007.

Glendon, Mary Ann. *Rights Talk: The Impoverishment of Political Discourse.* New York: Free Press, 1991.

Grant, Gerald. *The World We Created at Hamilton High.* Cambridge, MA: Harvard University Press, 1990.

Grumet, Jason. *City of Rivals.* Guilford CT: Lyons Press, 2014.

Haldane, Andrew. "The Dog and the Frisbee." Paper presented at the Federal Reserve Bank of Kansas City's 36th Economic Policy Symposium, Jackson Hole, WY, August 31, 2012. http://www.kansascityfed.org/publicat/sympos/2012/ah.pdf.

Hamilton, Alexander, James Madison, and John Jay. *The Federalist Papers.* New York: Modern Library, 2001.

Hammond, Kenneth R. *Human Judgment and Social Policy.* Oxford: Oxford University Press, 1996.

Harford, Tim. *Adapt: Why Success Always Starts with Failure.* New York: Farrar, Straus and Giroux, 2011.

Harrison, Lawrence E., and Samuel P. Huntington. *Culture Matters: How Values Shape Human Progress.* New York: Basic Books, 2000.

Havel, Václav. *The Art of the Impossible: Politics as Morality in Practice.* New York: Knopf, 1997.

Hayek, Friedrich A. *The Constitution of Liberty.* Chicago: University of Chicago Press, 1960.

———. *The Road to Serfdom.* Chicago: University of Chicago Press, 2007.

Heineman, Robert A. *Authority and the Liberal Tradition: From Hobbes to Rorty.* 2nd ed. New Brunswick, NJ: Transaction, 1994.

Hertogh, Marc. "Through the Eyes of Bureaucrats: How Front-Line Officials Understand Administrative Justice." In *Administrative Justice in Context,* edited by Michael Adler. Oxford: Hart, 2010.

Holmes, Oliver Wendell, Jr. *The Common Law.* Clark, NJ: Lawbook Exchange, 2005.

Holmes, Oliver Wendell, Jr. "Law in Science and Science in Law." *Harvard Law Review* 12 (1899): 443.

Howard, Philip K. "Civil Service Reform: Reassert the President's Constitutional Authority." *The American Interest,* January 28, 2017.

———. *The Collapse of the Common Good.* New York: Ballantine, 2002.

———. *The Death of Common Sense: How Law Is Suffocating America.* New York: Random House, 1994.

————. "History of American Law since 1968." In *Oxford Companion to American Law*, edited by Kermit L. Hall. New York: Oxford University Press, 2002.

————. *Life Without Lawyers*. New York: W. W. Norton, 2009.

————. *The Rule of Nobody*. New York: W. W. Norton, 2014.

————. "Two Years Not Ten Years." New York: Common Good, 2015.

Hummel, Ralph P. *The Bureaucratic Experience: The Post-modern Challenge*. 5th ed. Armonk, NY: M. E. Sharpe, 2008.

Jackson, Philip W., Robert E. Boostrom, and David T. Hansen. *The Moral Life of Schools*. San Francisco: Jossey-Bass, 1998.

James, William. *Writings, 1878–1899*. Edited by Gerald E. Myers. New York: Library of America, 1992.

Kagan, Robert A. *Adversarial Legalism: The American Way of Law*. Cambridge, MA: Harvard University Press, 2003.

Kaiser, Robert G. *Act of Congress: How America's Essential Institution Works, and How It Doesn't*. New York: Knopf, 2013.

————. *So Damn Much Money: The Triumph of Lobbying and the Corrosion of American Government*. New York: Knopf, 2009.

Kaufman, Herbert. *The Forest Ranger: A Study in Administrative Behavior*. 1960. Repr. Washington, DC: RFF Press, 2006.

Kelman, Steven. *Procurement and Public Management: The Fear of Discretion and the Quality of Government Performance*. Washington, DC: AEI Press, 1990.

Kennan, George F. *Around the Cragged Hill: A Personal and Political Philosophy*. New York: W. W. Norton, 1993.

Klein, Gary. *Intuition at Work: Why Developing Your Gut Instinct Will Make You Better at What You Do*. New York: Currency, 2004.

Kolakowski, Leszek. *Modernity on Endless Trial*. Chicago: University of Chicago Press, 1990.

Lacey, Nicola. "Jurisprudence of Discretion." In *The Uses of Discretion*, edited by Keith Hawkins. Oxford Socio-Legal Studies. Oxford: Clarendon, 1992.

Lasch, Christopher. *The Revolt of the Elites*. New York: W. W. Norton, 1996.

Lawrence-Lightfoot, Sara. *The Good High School: Portraits of Character and Culture*. New York: Basic Books, 1983.

Lessig, Lawrence. *Republic, Lost: How Money Corrupts Congress—and a Plan to Stop It*. New York: Twelve, 2011.

Levin, Yuval. *The Fractured Republic*. New York: Basic Books, 2016.

Light, Paul C. *A Government Ill Executed: The Decline of the Federal Service and How to Reverse It*. Cambridge, MA: Harvard University Press, 2008.

———. *Thickening Government: Federal Hierarchy and the Diffusion of Accountability*. Washington, DC: Brookings Institution Press, 1995.

Lilla, Mark. *The Once and Future Liberal*. New York: HarperCollins, 2017.

Lipsky, Michael. *Street-Level Bureaucracy: Dilemmas of the Individual in Public Services*. New York: Russell Sage Foundation, 1980.

Locke, John. *The Second Treatise on Civil Government*. Amherst, NY: Prometheus, 1986.

Lukianoff, Greg, and Jonathan Haidt. *The Coddling of the American Mind*. New York: Penguin, 2018.

MacIntyre, Alasdair C. *After Virtue: A Study in Moral Theory*. Notre Dame, IN: University of Notre Dame Press, 1984.

Mann, Thomas, and Norman Ornstein. *The Broken Branch*. Oxford: Oxford University Press, 2008.

———. *It's Even Worse Than It Looks*. New York: Basic Books, 2016.

Maxeiner, James R. *Failures of American Civil Justice in International Perspective*. Cambridge: Cambridge University Press, 2011.

———. *Failures of American Lawmaking in Historical and Comparative Perspectives*. Cambridge: Cambridge University Press, 2018.

Maynard-Moody, Steven, and Michael C. Musheno. *Cops, Teachers, Counselors: Stories from the Front Lines of Public Service*. Ann Arbor: University of Michigan Press, 2003.

Merton, Robert K. "Bureaucratic Structure and Personality." *Social Forces* 18, no. 4 (May 1940).

Merton, Robert K., Ailsa P. Gray, Barbara Hockey, and Hanan C. Selvin, eds. *Reader in Bureaucracy*. Glencoe, IL: Free Press, 1952.

Micklethwait, John, and Adrian Wooldridge. *The Fourth Revolution: The Global Race to Reinvent the State*. New York: Penguin Press, 2014.

Mill, John Stuart. *On Liberty*. Edited by David Bromwich and George Kateb. New Haven: Yale University Press, 2003.

Moulton, Lord John Fletcher. "Law and Manners." *Atlantic Monthly*, July 1924.

Muller, Jerry Z. *The Tyranny of Metrics*. Princeton: Princeton University Press, 2018.

Niebuhr, Reinhold. *The Essential Reinhold Niebuhr: Selected Essays and Addresses*. Edited by Robert McAfee Brown. New Haven: Yale University Press, 1986.

———. *Moral Man and Immoral Society: A Study in Ethics and Politics*. Rev. ed. New York: Scribner, 1960.

Nisbet, Robert. *Twilight of Authority*. Carmel, IN: Liberty Fund, 2000.

Nonet, Philippe, and Philip Selznick. *Law and Society in Transition: Toward Responsive Law*. New York: Harper & Row, 1978.

Noonan, Kathleen G., Charles F. Sabel, and William H. Simon. "Legal Accountability in the Service-Based Welfare State." *Law & Social Inquiry* 34, no. 3 (Summer 2009).

O'Neill, Onora. *A Question of Trust: The BBC Reith Lectures 2002*. Cambridge: Cambridge University Press, 2002.

OECD (Organisation for Economic Co-operation and Development). "Implementing Administrative Simplification in OECD Countries: Experiences and Challenges." http://www.oecd.org/mena/govern ance/37026688.pdf.

———. "Recommendation of the Council on Regulatory Policy and Governance." 2012. http://www.oecd.org/gov/regulatory-policy/49990817.pdf.

———. Regulatory Enforcement and Inspections, OECD Best Practice Principles for Regulatory Policy. OECD Publishing, 2014.

———. Regulatory Reform in the United States. Paris: OECD, 1999.

Olson, Walter. *The Litigation Explosion: What Happened When America Unleashed the Lawsuit*. New York: Truman Talley, 1992.

Peters, Charles. *How Washington Really Works*. New York: Basic Books, 1992.

Phelps, Edmund. *Mass Flourishing*. Princeton: Princeton University Press, 2015.

Polanyi, Michael. *Personal Knowledge: Towards a Post-Critical Philosophy*. Chicago: University of Chicago Press, 1958.

Polybius. *The Histories*. Translated by Mortimer Chambers. New York: Washington Square Press, 1966.

Porter, Theodore M. *Trust in Numbers: The Pursuit of Objectivity in Science and Public Life.* Princeton: Princeton University Press, 1995.

Putnam, Robert D. *Bowling Alone: The Collapse and Revival of American Community.* New York: Simon & Schuster, 2000.

Raban, Ofer. "The Fallacy of Legal Certainty: Why Vague Legal Standards May Be Better for Capitalism and Liberalism." *Boston University Public Interest Law Journal* 19, no. 2 (Spring 2010).

Rauch, Jonathan. *Government's End: Why Washington Stopped Working.* New York: PublicAffairs, 1999.

Raz, Joseph. "Legal Principles and the Limits of Law." *Yale Law Journal* 81, no. 5 (April 1972).

Reich, Robert. *The Common Good.* New York: Knopf, 2018.

Rohr, John A. "Professionalism, Legitimacy, and the Constitution." *Public Administration Quarterly* 8, no. 4 (Winter 1985).

Romer, Paul M. "Process, Responsibility, and Myron's Law." In *In the Wake of the Crisis: Leading Economists Reassess Economic Policy,* edited by Olivier J. Blanchard, David Romer, A. Michael Spence, and Joseph E. Stiglitz. Cambridge, MA: MIT Press, 2012.

Rose, Mike. *The Mind at Work: Valuing the Intelligence of the American Worker.* New York: Viking, 2004.

Rubin, Edward L. "Discretion and Its Discontents." *Chicago-Kent Law Review* 72 (1997).

Sabel, Charles F., and William H. Simon. "Minimalism and Experimentalism in the Administrative State." *Georgetown Law Journal* 100, no. 1 (2011).

Sandel, Michael J. *Democracy's Discontent: America in Search of a Public Philosophy.* Cambridge, MA: Belknap Press, 1996.

Sandler, Ross, and David Schoenbrod. *Democracy by Decree: What Happens When Courts Run Government.* New Haven: Yale University Press, 2003.

Schaar, John H. "Liberty/Authority/Community in the Political Thought of John Winthrop." *Political Theory* 19, no. 4 (November 1991).

Schlesinger, Arthur M., Jr. *The Age of Jackson.* Boston: Back Bay Books, 1988.

———. *The Disuniting of America: Reflections on a Multicultural Society.* New York: W. W. Norton, 1998.

Schoenbrod, David. *DC Confidential.* New York: Encounter Books, 2017.

Schuck, Peter. *Why Government Fails So Often*. Princeton: Princeton University Press, 2014.

Schwartz, Barry, and Kenneth Sharpe. *Practical Wisdom: The Right Way to Do the Right Thing*. New York: Riverhead Books, 2010.

Scott, James C. *Seeing Like a State: How Certain Schemes to Improve the Human Condition Have Failed*. New Haven: Yale University Press, 1999.

Simon, William H. "Legality, Bureaucracy, and Class in the Welfare System." *Yale Law Journal* 92, no. 7 (June 1983).

———. "Solving Problems vs. Claiming Rights: The Pragmatist Challenge to Legal Liberalism." *William and Mary Law Review* 46, no. 1 (2004).

———. "Toyota Jurisprudence: Legal Theory and Rolling Rule Regimes." Columbia Public Law Research Paper 04-79, October 2004.

Simon, Yves. *Philosophy of Democratic Government*. Notre Dame, IN: University of Notre Dame Press, 1993.

Slater, Philip. *The Pursuit of Loneliness: American Culture at the Breaking Point*. Boston: Beacon Press, 1990.

Solzhenitsyn, Aleksandr. *Solzhenitsyn at Harvard: The Address, Twelve Early Responses, and Six Later Reflections*. Edited by Ronald Berman. Washington, DC: Ethics and Public Policy Center, 1980.

Sternberg, Robert J., George B. Forsythe, Jennifer Hedlund, and Joseph A. Horvath. *Practical Intelligence in Everyday Life*. Cambridge: Cambridge University Press, 2000.

Stewart, Richard B. "Madison's Nightmare." *University of Chicago Law Review* 57, no. 2 (Spring 1990).

———. "The Reformation of American Administrative Law." 88 *Harvard Law Review* 1669 (1975).

Stuntz, William J. *The Collapse of American Criminal Justice*. Cambridge, MA: Belknap Press, 2011.

Sunstein, Cass. *Risk and Reason: Safety, Law, and the Environment*. Chicago: University of Chicago Press, 2002.

———. *Simpler: The Future of Government*. New York: Simon & Schuster, 2013.

Taleb, Nassim. *Antifragile: Things That Gain from Disorder*. New York: Random House, 2012.

Tamanaha, Brian Z. *On the Rule of Law: History, Politics, Theory*. Cambridge: Cambridge University Press, 2004.

Teles, Steven M. "Kludgeocracy: The American Way of Policy." New America Foundation. December 10, 2012. http://newamerica.net/publications/policy/kludgeocracy_the_ american_way_of_policy.

Tocqueville, Alexis de. *Democracy in America*. Edited by Phillips Bradley. 2 vols. New York: Vintage, 1990.

———. *The Old Regime and the French Revolution*. Translated by Stuart Gilbert. New York: Doubleday, 1983.

Van Riper, Paul P. *History of the United States Civil Service*. Evanston, IL: Row, Peterson, 1958.

Vance, J. D. *Hillbilly Elegy: A Memoir of a Family and Culture in Crisis*. New York: HarperCollins, 2016.

Waldron, Jeremy. "The Rule of Law and the Importance of Procedure." In *Getting to the Rule of Law*, edited by James E. Fleming. Nomos: Yearbook of the American Society for Political and Legal Philosophy 50. New York: New York University Press, 2011.

———. "Thoughtfulness and the Rule of Law." NYU School of Law, Public Law Research Paper No. 11-13, February 10, 2011. http://papers.ssrn.com/sol3/papers.cfm?abstract_id= 1759550.

———. "Vagueness in Law and Language: Some Philosophical Issues." *California Law Review* 82, no. 3 (May 1994).

White, Leonard D. *The Federalists: A Study in Administrative History*. New York: Macmillan, 1948.

Wildavsky, Aaron. *Searching for Safety*. New Brunswick, NJ: Transaction Publishers, 1988.

Will, George F. *Statecraft as Soulcraft: What Government Does*. New York: Simon & Schuster, 1983.

Zakaria, Fareed. *The Future of Freedom*. New York: W. W. Norton, 2007.

INDEX

Page numbers followed by *n* indicate notes.